Disss-co (A Fragment)

DISTANZ

Disss-co (A Fragment)

Douglas Crimp
with Henrik Olesen

KONTEXT

Contents

"Guy Hocquenghem visited New York and stayed with me in my loft on Chambers Street, and one night while I was out, he read what I'd written. When I returned later, he said to me that such straightforward description of gay culture was just the sort of thing that gay activists should be writing."

— Douglas Crimp

Editor's Note

Matthias Kliefoth

Douglas Crimp's essay *Disss-co (A Fragment)* marks an important beginning of an era that almost seems clear today. Writing means activism. Disco is freedom. The body is an asset and outlet for identities.

Crimp's honest, ambivalent writings on representation and critique remain an uncontested milestone in the debate over queer aesthetics. The essay, at first never intended to be published and found by his friend and intellectual companion Guy Hocquenghem, reads as a primer to Crimp's pioneering studies of gay subcultures in New York's underground scene and beyond. Henrik Olesen's work *Lack of Information* displays and orders the artist's research on the suppression of queer refugees to Europe already in 2001, years before European borders were questioned once more by a world shifting its understanding of religion, identity, and geography. In the dark light of today's renewed repression of sexual minorities and ethnic subcultural communities, neither Crimp's text nor Olesen's work have lost any of their relevance, intersecting with each other in their brilliant ways of looking at subcultural codes and liberation from hegemonic structures.

We have chosen not to translate the essay nor to alter the textual layer of Olesen's work in order to retain their intimate spirit. We have also decided to convert the endnotes in Crimp's original text into footnotes since they are an essential part of his observations on the freedom of dance culture, which remains an integral aspect of queer political and body positive liberation.

With this first book in our series *KONTEXT* we are excited to create a format that combines textual and visual artistic practices. Featuring commissioned and reissued essays and experimental writing, the publication series seeks to examine current debates and their perspectives through both academic and creative writing in dialogue with contemporary art.

Disss-co (A Fragment)

Douglas Crimp

Among the papers from the mid-1970s that I've kept all these years are a few pages of something I'd begun writing about disco. They remain in a dog-eared folder marked "projects." Everything else in the folder is art-related, including a proposal for a book on contemporary art. I'm amazed now at the hubris of believing I could write a full-scale book about "art from Minimal sculpture forward," but pleasantly surprised to see evidence that I was thinking about contemporary art under the rubric of postmodernism as early as 1976. "The starting point," I wrote, "is to discuss the important shift from Modernism to Post-Modernism."[1]

The few pages on disco are the only ones in this folder that I'd looked at in the intervening years; the reason is that they carry a particular sentimental value. Around the time I wrote them, Guy Hocquenghem visited New York and stayed with me in my loft on Chambers Street, and one night while I was out he read what I'd written. When I returned later, he said to me

1. A British graduate student recently e-mailed me to ask how I came to characterize the artists in my 1977 Artists Space exhibition *Pictures* as "postmodernist" in the revised version of the catalogue essay, published in *October* in 1979. Since I hadn't used that term in the original essay, he wondered, what had transpired in the meantime? When had I begun to think about postmodernism? Was it through my association with other *October* critics such as Craig Owens? Did I take the term from architectural discourse, where by 1978 it was used fairly regularly? I couldn't remember. But now, reading my book project dating from 1975 or 1976, I find the word *postmodernism*. See Douglas Crimp, *Pictures: An Exhibition of the Work of Troy Brauntuch, Jack Goldstein, Sherrie Levine, Robert Longo, Philip Smith* (New York: Artists Space, 1977); and Douglas Crimp, "Pictures," *October*, no. 8 (Spring 1979), 75–88.

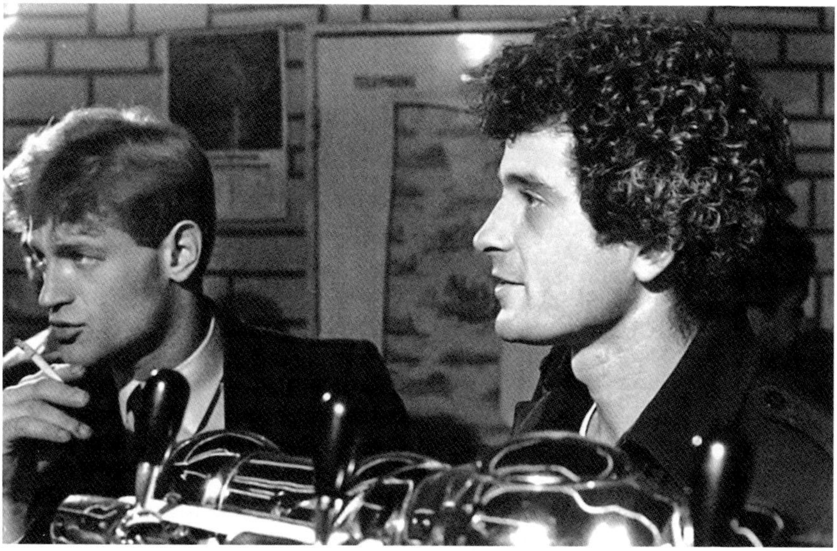

Piotr Stanislas (left) and Guy Hocquenghem (right) in Guy Hocquenghem and Lionel Soukaz, *Race d'Ep!*, black-and-white and color, sound, 95 min.

that such a straightforward description of gay culture was just the sort of thing that gay activists should be writing. I was embarrassed that Guy had found and read the pages. I'm self-conscious about my unfinished writing; this was not at all the sort of writing I did professionally and thus had any confidence in; and, though younger than I, Guy was both a heartthrob and an idol. Christian sent Guy my way in winter 1974. "Take much care of Guy, he is a darling," Christian wrote, and indeed he was and I did. He stayed with me, sharing my bed, for a few months. We went dancing most nights at Peter Rabbit's, a tiny gay bar with a largely black clientele and a great jukebox on the corner of West and Tenth Streets.

While still in his midtwenties, Guy had been a founder of FHAR (Front Homosexuel d'Action Révolutionnaire, the French gay-liberation organization) and a year later, in 1972, published *Homosexual Desire.*[2] Although he'd subsequently published a second gay-liberation tract, *L'Après-mai des faunes,* and would eventually write his own descriptions of gay life in *Le Gay voyage,* he was now turning his attention to fiction. He had recently published *Fin de section,* a collection of short stories, and begun work on his first novel, *Love in Relief.*[3]

2. Guy Hocquenghem, *Le Désir homosexuel* (Paris: Jean-Pierre Delarge, 1972), translated into English by Daniella Dangoor, preface by Jeffrey Weeks (London: Allison & Busby, 1978); reprinted with an introduction by Michael Moon (Durham, NC: Duke University Press, 1993).

3. Guy Hocquenghem, *L'Après mai des faunes: Volutions* (Paris: Grasset, 1974); *Le Gay voyage: guide homosexual des grandes métropoles* (Paris: Albin Michel, 1980); *Fin de section* (Paris: Christian Bourgois, 1975); *Love in Relief,* trans. Michael Whistler (New York: Seahorse Press, 1986). For more on Hocquenghem, see Bill Marshall, *Guy Hocquenghem: Beyond Gay Identity* (Durham: Duke University Press, 1997).

Perhaps the story-like way I begin the fragment on disco is what appealed to Guy.

The sun seemed unnaturally bright when we opened the door and walked out onto lower Broadway. Steven adjusted the pitch-black, wrap-around sunglasses that he'd put on in the lobby. As we walked down Houston Street toward the Village, our bodies still gyrated, slowing our walk to a rhythmic amble. Moving at all was slightly painful and yet felt inevitable, as if the music had been absorbed by our muscles, especially the obliques, and would go on propelling that uncontrollable back-and-forth hip-swaying forever. On the way up Bedford Street to Seventh Avenue, two guys passed us. When one was right next to him, Steven drew out under his breath in a reverent whisper, *"Disss-co."* He gave it the same whooshing, electronic sound as the feedback drone that lingered in our ears, muting the sounds of the early Sunday morning. The two men smiled knowingly. There was no question where we were all coming from.

"It was *hot* tonight," Steven said. "It was really crazy, though. At first it was like that night at 12 West when we left so early. Creeps everywhere you looked, plaguing you. And you couldn't get into it. The lights were sobright, and the music was weird. Then all of a sudden the music got real hot, they turned off those bright lights, everything went red and blue, and everybody was gorgeous—just big, hot, butch muscle numbers. Suddenly it was a different night. Then, after that real hot set, the music had no beat. Remember, I kept asking you if the music had a beat. I couldn't get into it. And I couldn't tell if Bobby liked it or not, but he kept dancing. He's a little bopper, Bobby. He just bops around. He's hot. You discoed good, babe. It was real good disco. *Disss-co.*"

Steven's conversation continues like that for at least a whole day after Saturday-night disco. A running analysis of the night before, the night that's really morning, beginning about 1 a.m. and lasting until 7 or 8. Of course, that's not counting the preparation, which begins early Saturday. Getting your disco act together. Finding a member to go with. Eating lots of protein, but early in the day. Resting up. Deciding what drugs to take and what clothes to wear. The clothes are particularly important because, apart from wanting the right look, you have to figure out how much you can comfortably shed or allow to get drenched in sweat without its bring- ing you down. At least until about 5:30, when nothing can bring you down. At that point, the music is always good, there's plenty of room on the dance floor, and only the serious discoers are left. But best of all your body has quit resisting. It has unstoppable momentum. That is the one thing about disco comparable to any other experience. It's like what happens in distance running or swimming. You pass a point where you're beyond tired, beyond pain, beyond even thinking about stopping, thinking only that this could go on forever and you'd love it. It's pure ecstasy. Nothing matters but disco, and nothing—not sex, not food, not sleep, nothing—is better.

The place Steven and I had just come from is called Flamingo. One of the first and most elaborate of the new private dance clubs, Flamingo has been operating for two seasons. That is something of a longevity record for gay discos, which usually last only about six months before a new and better place to dance comes along. There are several reasons for Flamingo's staying power. One is that Michael Fesco, the owner, has a loyal following among the A-list gay crowd. And Fesco shrewdly closes the club every spring, just as the devotees begin to tire of the routine. Most of the Flamingo crowd spend their summer weekends on Fire Island anyway. But more important, membership at Flamingo is by invitation only, which guarantees the clubby atmosphere this crowd loves. The feeling that the club is special, exclusive, the *best,* is essential to a good disco. Membership costs forty-five dollars per season; a member pays five dollars at the door and his guests pay seven dollars. What that gets you is juice, soda, coffee, fresh fruit, and stale doughnuts, which nobody much cares for. There's no liquor, and nobody cares about that at all. What the price of admission really gets you is the most perfect dancing environment yet, and the ingredients for that are very precarious.

Flamingo is located in a big, anonymous loft building on the northeast edge of SoHo, where on a Saturday night there's nobody else around. There's no sign in front, not even a lighted doorway. Going there for the first time feels like an initiation into a secret society. Gay men love the kinds of rituals that make what they do seem secretive, forbidden. (As if the whole world wouldn't realize Flamingo was there from the pulsating of the entire building—in fact, the building houses two discos; the other one is the Gallery—and the endless line of cabs pulling up in front from midnight to 6 a.m. New York taxi drivers could tell you a thing or two about forbidden places in New York.)

You walk through the uninviting entrance into a completely dark foyer where you can vaguely perceive that there are a few people shuffling around. Then a flashlight lights up and you put your membership card in its beam. You've passed the first test. You go through the doors at the back of the lobby to the stairway. There are two official-looking, if a bit stoned, attendants there to check your membership number off in a ledger, write down the number of guests with you (you're allowed two), and write out a bill—nineteen dollars for three. You then wait in line to go upstairs. This is the tensest part of the evening because you can hear the music coming from upstairs, and they're usually playing one of your favorite songs, so you know you'll miss dancing to it. At the top of the stairs, which are usually crowded with anxious, whispery guys, you pay your money and get your hand stamped with ink that glows under black light. Finally, you're in, but still not ready for the dance floor. There's another line at the coat check, which takes *forever,* because you have to decide there and then how much to take off, and there's a feverish shuffling of necessities from the pockets of shed clothing to pockets in what you're still wearing: joints of dust, poppers, inhaler, downs, cigarettes, matches, coke, coke spoon, ethyl chloride (if you're a rag queen). If you're smart, you do all of this at home, but that means making the difficult decisions before you've got the feel of the place.

The next problem is getting into it, but that's not usually severe. Sometimes when you arrive late the dance floor is so crowded that it's difficult to penetrate, and the energy level is already so high that it's alienating. There are people acting really wild and ecstatic, and completely out of

The text ends there—at the bottom of a typewritten page, but not quite at the end of a line, so I don't think there's a page missing; I think I just stopped. The next page is the beginning of a brief history of disco:

> Discotheques are nothing new. They came in during the 1960s, when people realized that good dance music was too dependent on studio effects to be reproduced by a live band. They were part of that very brief episode when London—King's Road and Chelsea especially—was synonymous with hip. They had names like Annabelle's and Arthur, and later the Electric Circus and Hippopotamus. They were private, or at least exclusive. They were expensive. They were straight. And now those places belong to bygone days.
>
> The new discotheques bear very little resemblance to those places. In fact, they aren't even heirs to that tradition. Flamingo, 12 West, Infinity, the Loft, and Frankenstein are gay. Their predecessors are different kinds of places, still in some ways reflected in the new discos. These include the Sanctuary, a late-1960s discotheque in an unused church on Forty-Third Street; the Firehouse, the headquarters of the Gay Activists' Alliance, whose engine house became a dance hall on weekends;[4] and the Tenth Floor, a private juice bar in a West Twenties loft. What all of these places had in common are traits of pariah culture: they were located in out-of-the-way neighborhoods in quickly refurbished spaces with the palpable feeling of being susceptible to a bust at any moment. You always knew that their days were numbered, that they would be shut down by the law, burnt down, or just abandoned for a new and better place to dance.

And there are a few pages that suggest a more analytical project titled "Disco: Technologized Pleasure." One of these begins:

4. Richie Rivera, who had DJed at the Firehouse, became one of the DJs at Flamingo in 1977, after having worked in the interim at the Sandpiper in Fire Island Pines and at the Anvil in New York.

What would it be like if we were able to somehow produce ecstasy synthetically? [The psychoactive drug MDMA, popularly known as ecstasy, came into use as a party drug only in the 1980s.] If we were able to just plug ourselves into a machine that would produce pleasure? Is ecstasy something that can exist in a pure state, apart from some interpersonal context, from a connection of the ecstatic moment with a whole matrix of feeling about, let's say, another person with whom that ecstasy might be linked?

Another begins:

I want to describe the disco experience in a way that might convey what is extraordinary about it and also show how it is symptomatic of a wider experience of pleasure in our society, a mode of experience that is both terrifying and overwhelmingly powerful.

When I first went to the new kind of discos a few years ago I was struck by the conformity of the people there, conformity that goes well beyond the stylistic similarities of people in a demimonde. It was not only a question of similar hairstyles or that everyone had the same mustache. The most striking aspect of the similarity was that these people have identical bodies, and these bodies are also strikingly different from other bodies. They seem to be honed for a particular activity, maybe a fairly athletic form of sex. In fact, that activity is dancing, or what has become known as dancing. These bodies have been made into dancing machines.

Finally there are a few notes:

Place: Synthetic materials, industrial gloss, futuristic, spacey, technologized surfaces and lighting. Enormous plants and bowls of fruit appear as if technologically produced, having no similarity to natural objects. Views through doorways to the outside world are extremely disturbing. Views of reality look

> unreal, nightmarish, tacky. Going outside is always a shock, and it takes days to readjust to ugly reality.
>
> People: Synthetically produced bodies using bodybuilding machines and protein supplements. Bodies moving en masse, like cogs in a machine.

What I wrote in 1975 or 1976 seems fairly obvious now. If there is anything interesting about it, it's that there was a time when all this appeared so new and astonishing—and so peculiarly gay, which is what must have interested Guy. The mention of "synthetically produced bodies" provides one clue as to why: Nautilus had just come out with their first line of machines. The innovation of the Nautilus was that it isolated a muscle group and, through the use of a logarithmic spiral cam around which the chain is wrapped, made the load of weight on the muscles consistent through the entire range of exercise motion. This meant that energy expended in working out was used efficiently to produce results. Nowadays, of course, every decent health club has a great many brand-name variations of these workout machines, but in the 1960s and early 1970s bodybuilding still consisted of simple calisthenics, free weights, and Universal stack weight machines, and serious bodybuilding was pretty much limited to the subculture of bodybuilding contests. Arnold Schwarzenegger was the first bodybuilder to become well-known beyond the subculture—as a bodybuilder, that is, rather than as a fitness-program huckster like Charles Atlas or a sword-and-sandals movie actor like Steve Reeves or Mickey Hargitay. Schwarzenegger is one of the competition bodybuilders featured in Charles Gaines and George Butler's book *Pumping Iron,* published in 1974, and he became the star of the film of the same title, released in 1977. To help finance the film, Butler persuaded the Whitney Museum to host a promotional event, billed as *Articulate Muscle: The Male Body in Art.* Candice Bergen was hired to photograph it for the *Today* show, and Elliott Erwitt did so on his own. His pictures show what an unexpected success the event was—more than twenty-five hundred people showed up, most of them gay men, judging from their looks. A panel of art historians, moderated by *New York Times* critic Vicki Goldberg, watched three Mr. Olympia contestants pose and then conducted "a long panel discussion and slide show of the human physique in art and as art through the ages. Most people seemed angry or bored. Very few people paid attention." But for Schwarzenegger, it was "like going to heaven."[5]

Sometime before writing the disco fragment I had become friendly with *New Yorker* humor writer Veronica Geng, who, among other quirky interests, was a follower of bodybuilding, and she had gotten to know Schwarzenegger and told me about him.[6] Veronica was also a devotee of New York City Ballet, to which she also introduced me, and she managed to combine her enthusiasm for these two types of bodies, shaped by

5. Ian Frazier, "Muscles at the Whitney," *New Yorker*, March 22, 1976, 27.

6. Geng wrote an article about bodybuilding for *Ms. Magazine* in 1975. (Veronica Geng, "Muscle over Mind," *Ms.*, October 1975, 24–30.)

rigorous daily routines, by introducing Schwarzenegger to City Ballet principal Peter Martins with a view to getting the dancer to assist the bodybuilder with his posing technique.

It was around this time that large numbers of gay men began going to gyms. The gyms we went to were either YMCAs or hard-core bodybuilding clubs, since well-appointed fitness centers were still in the future. I joined the West Side Y in 1974; that's where I first encountered gay men whom I recognized from Flamingo pumping up their muscles on Nautilus machines.[7] If you compare the "natural" musculature on the guys in photographs of the 1970s New York gay scene, you'll see why I was so amazed at the "synthetically produced bodes," the "dancing machines" I saw at the disco. I vividly remember the first time I took notice of a gay man with disproportionately large pectoral muscles. It was on Fire Island in summer 1973. He was a very good-looking guy named Frank who always came shirtless to tea dance at the Botel in the Pines, and my friends and I

7. "Almost every YMCA in America has a weight room, and all of the ones I know about (with a few exceptions, like the big Y on Central Park West where the faggots will track you to the shower with their heads down like they were following a spoor) are wonderful places to train." Charles Gaines, *Pumping Iron: The Art and Sport of Bodybuilding* (New York: Simon and Schuster, 1974), 27–28. The homophobia here is typical of the book's text, no doubt as a reaction formation, but here from the book's preface is the stated reason: "Almost since its beginnings here [in the United States], bodybuilding has advertised itself with consummate tackiness, confining itself to the back pages of pulp magazines and, in the national consciousness, to the same shadowy corners occupied by dildos and raincoat exhibitionists. Unflattering myths developed early here. And the composite picture that seems to have emerged from them, of bodybuilders as narcissistic, coordinatively helpless muscleheads with suspect sexual preferences, has done little to promote the sport. Part of what we have tried to do is to demonstrate that this is an inaccurate picture." 8.

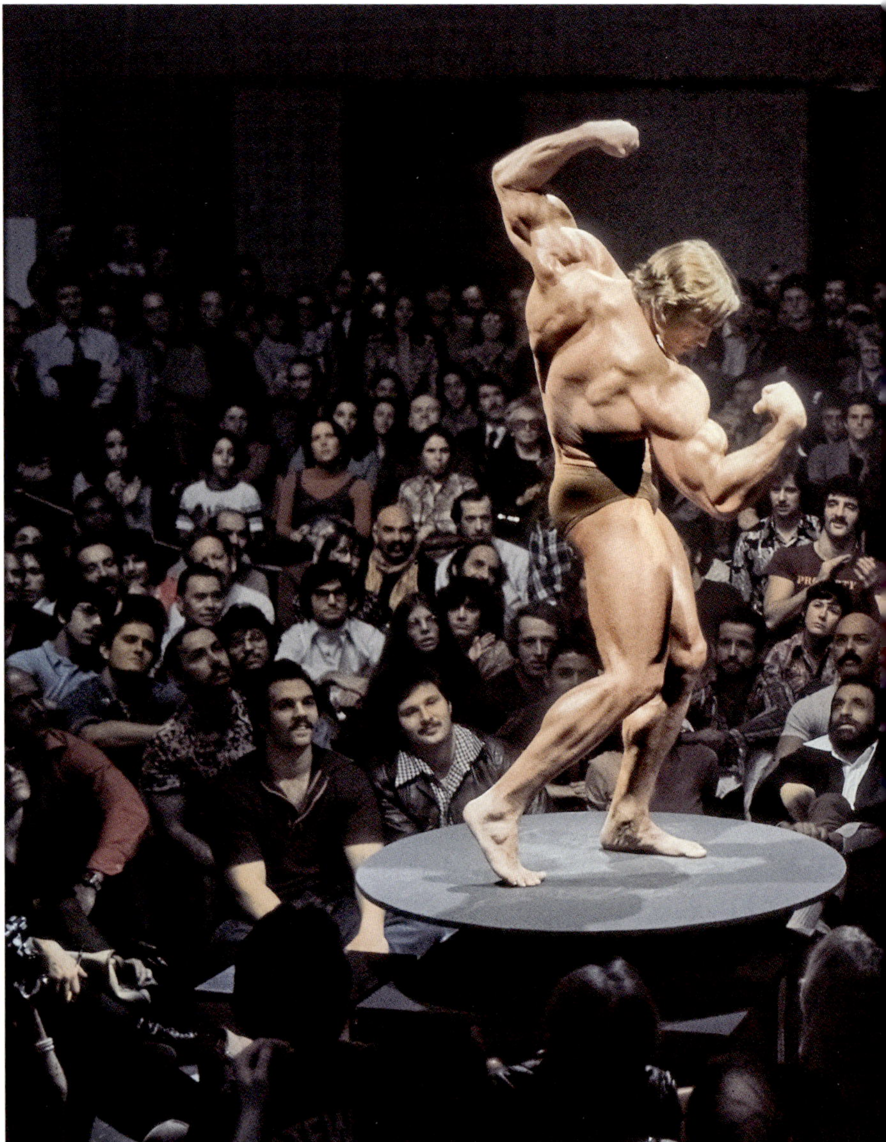

Arnold Schwarzenegger posing during the event *Articulate Muscle: The Male Body in Art*, Whitney Museum of American Art, New York, February 25, 1976. Photo by Elliott Erwitt/Magnum Photos

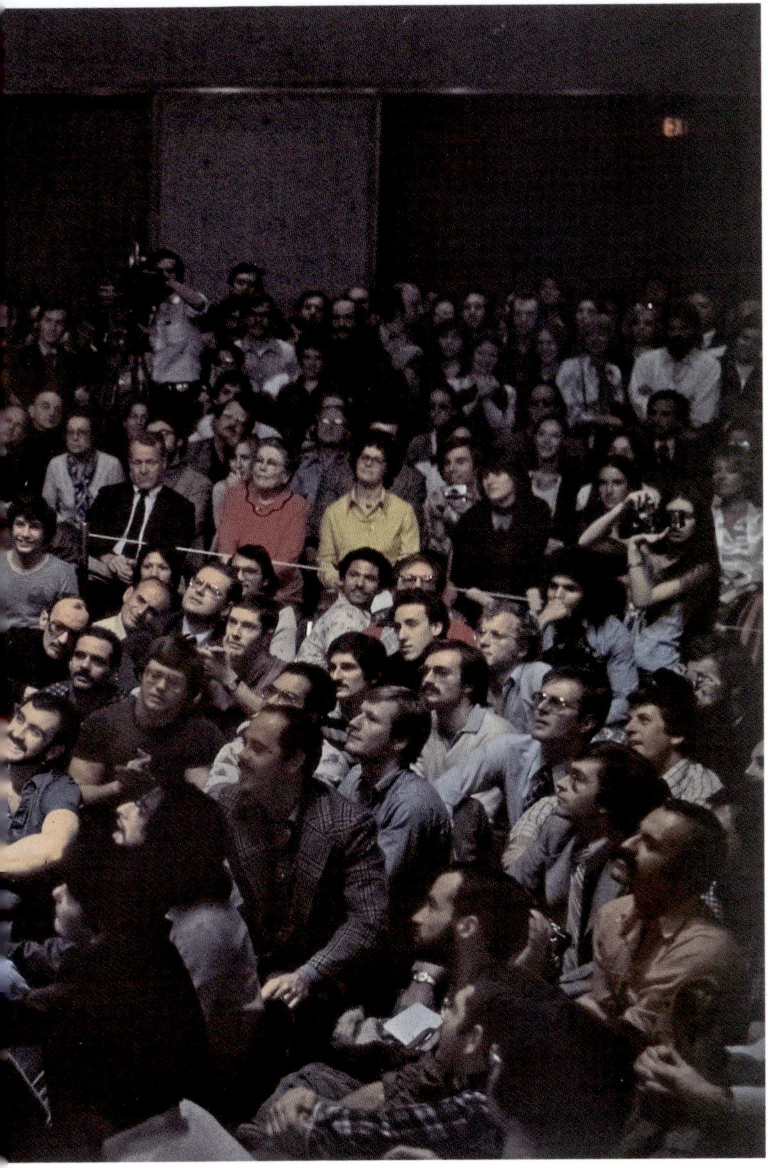

couldn't stop staring at and talking about his massive pecs. I guess I'd never before fully recognized the sexual appeal of that part of a man's anatomy; it took a chest overdeveloped by weight training to make me focus on it so fetishistically. Within a short five years, sculpted pectoral muscles had become one of the main attributes of gay male desirability, and Flamingo institutionalized it. Toward the conclusion of his history of 1970s disco, *Love Saves the Day,* Tim Lawrence writes that Flamingo was starting to be "driven by an increasingly high dose of self-absorption":

> The launch of the first annual "Tetas" (Spanish for "tit") contest—a variation of the female topless dance—in October 1978 confirmed the drive toward vanity and bodily display, with the chest reigning in the new temples of butch, and the month Nathan Fain noted that Flamingo members "can barely stand how handsome they are, the first confirmed case of group narcissism on record." [8]

Gay men's overdeveloped breasts eventually came to be called disco tits. My project on disco—such as it was—was probably an attempt to work through my ambivalence about the new scene. I wasn't a member at Flamingo; I didn't measure up to its standard of physical beauty, and I felt excluded by its cliquishness

8. Tim Lawrence, *Love Saves the Day: A History of American Dance Music Culture,* 1970–1979 (Durham, NC: Duke University Press, 2003), 424. Lawrence quotes Nathan Fain, writing at the time in the entertainment magazine *After Dark*. Flamingo's choice of tetas rather than pecs for the name of its annual contest suggests that something more than the chest was being fetishized: Latino men. Andrew Holleran's 1978 novel *Dancer from the Dance* makes this explicit.

and conformity. But I was also attracted to some of the guys I thought did meet the standard, and I felt happy to be there when I found a member to go with. Most of all, I had always loved to dance, starting with fifth-grade ballroom-dance classes; intensifying during my junior-high-school years, when I learned to jitterbug with my older sister's friends; intensifying still more when I easily picked up all the 1960s dance crazes from the twist and the Watusi to line dances like the Hully Gully (which would serve me well for learning the Hustle during my disco days); and intensifying most of all when the music, in the hands of the DJ, seemed to make my body move as if by remote control and manipulate my mood in ever-increasing rushes of pleasure. Of course, this last phase of dance loving was enhanced by drugs—everything from acid to angel dust, a tranquilizer so powerful and spatially disorienting that it was wise while high on it to stay in one place on the dance floor. (The "rag queens" I mention in the fragment on disco are what we called the guys who used ethyl chloride; they would soak a handkerchief in the chemical anesthetic and each put one end of it in his mouth to get high. You can see this in one of the disco sequences of William Friedkin's 1980 film *Cruising*.)

Drugs—always hard on me—were probably the major cause of my ambivalence. I'm one of those people made edgy and paranoid instead of mellow by pot. On an acid trip, I hallucinated being in the middle of a forest fire. Heroin made me throw up. Speed made me feel great for an hour and crash for twenty-four. Once on Fire Island, a group of us took mescaline before going into the water to play in the surf, got caught in a rip current, and just barely saved ourselves from drowning. I was tripping on hallucinogenic mushrooms at a party in Los Angeles when the police raided it. I took way too many drugs during the late 1960s and 1970s. I took them alone, with friends and boyfriends, at parties, for sex, for the "experience," but most of all I took them for disco. You can't really give yourself over to serious discoing without drugs. You need the incredible level of energy they give the illusion of supplying, and you need their disinhibiting quality to allow the music's beat to take over your body, inhabit it, make it move with no sense of volition. Without drugs, disco can be fun, but just fun.

I resisted disinhibition probably because I was trying to get serious about being an art critic right at the time I became a disco bunny. I fought the effect of the drugs I took. I thought at the disco. I thought, "Why are all these grown-up men acting like excited children? Why do I like this so much? How will I feel about this tomorrow?" Several years ago, I read a passage *of The Philosophy of Andy Warhol* that resonated with my disco experience. It's not about drugs or dancing, it's about sex, but the analogy works perfectly:

> Some people can have sex and really let their minds go blank and fill up with the sex; other people can never let their minds go blank and fill up with the sex, so while they're having

> the sex they're thinking, "Can this really be me? Am I really doing this? This is very strange. Five minutes ago I wasn't doing this. In a little while I won't be doing it. What would Mom say? How did people ever think of doing this?" So the first type of person—the type that can let their minds go blank and fill up with sex and not-think-about-it—is better off. The other type has to find something else to relax with and get lost in.[9]

I tried to resolve my disco ambivalence not by finding something else but by changing venues. I stopped going to Flamingo and shifted my loyalty to 12 West, which was a bit less A-list and a bit more diverse. Later I occasionally went to Paradise Garage, which was way more diverse, but by the time the Garage opened in 1977 I'd started graduate school and become the managing editor of *October,* and the demands of course work and running a quarterly journal interfered with my disco routine. Eventually I pretty much stopped going to the big, fabulous gay discos. I realized that in many ways I preferred the grungy little gay bars that had dance floors, like Crisco Disco and the Cock Ring. I could go at a more convenient hour any night of the week, never have to stand in line to get in, pay no admission, and still dance to music mixed by some of the best DJs spinning in New York. And unlike those at the "real" discos, the patrons of these places were into more than just dancing, which meant that my night often ended with one of them in my bed. Maybe I took Warhol's advice "to find something else to relax with and get lost in" after all.

9. Andy Warhol, *The Philosophy of Andy Warhol (From A to B and Back Again)* (New York: Harcourt Brace Jovanovich, 1975), 48–49.

The clearest sign to me that my disco project stemmed from my ambivalence is that I described Flamingo instead of 12 West. I thought of 12 West as my disco during my serious disco days, which in memory seem to stretch over the entire decade of the 1970s but must really have been the few years from 1974 to 1977. The dance floor at 12 West was not only bigger than Flamingo's but also much better designed. It was a square inscribed in another square, with triangular, stepped, carpeted platforms on three sides of the dance floor. (The fourth triangle that would have completed the square was only implied by the other three; the dance floor actually continued into the entrance lobby in one direction and a juice bar and lounge area in the other.) You could stand and dance in place on the platforms and look out over the dance floor at its sea of moving bodies, spotting friends or the attractive stranger you'd noticed earlier dancing next to you. At Flamingo, by contrast, the dance floor occupied one end of a long, narrow loft. It was approachable from only one side, and when the place was crowded there was never enough space between the sidewalls and the dance floor to make moving around it possible. The platforms at 12 West offered options. You could immerse yourself in the thick of dancing bodies, or you could stand slightly above and apart and take in the beauty of the multitude moving as one while dancing in place to the beat.

Another thing I liked about 12 West was that there were skylights above the dance floor, so when dancing 'til dawn you actually got to experience the dawn. I think this reduced the shock of moving from the synthetic, strobelit world of the disco to the diurnal streets outside. Day slowly broke over the dance floor, the crowd thinned, you danced a last dance or two, and as the sun really began to pour into the room you saw that your surroundings weren't so magical after all but just an old industrial space, and you were happy enough to return to your regular life.[10] The song I remember as my all-time disco favorite—Esther Phillips's disco cover of Dinah Washington's "What a Diff'rence a Day Makes"[11]—dates from when I began going to 12 West; reprised at dawn, the lyric might have been "What a diff'rence day makes." I was certainly being hyperbolic when I wrote in the fragment that it took "days to adjust to ugly reality." Regular hours, jobs and other quotidian responsibilities, and being surrounded by ordinary, mostly straight people who had no appreciation of the intensities of pleasure that disco afforded did take some adjustment, and it did take time for even a young,

10. Evidently others disagreed with my assessment of the effect of the skylights: "Back in the Village, the owners of 12 West discovered that they were having their own problems maintaining the 'cloak of nonthreatening anonymity' that was so important to gay men who were in the club but not quite out of the closet. 'We couldn't stay open too early [*sic*] because we had light coming through the skylight,' says owner Alan Harris. 'People would also begin to look very *gray* at eight in the morning.' Consequently the club started to close its doors at five, with [DJ] Tom Savarese winding up an hour later. 'Tom would stop promptly at six o'clock and go into a set of encores that would begin to bring the crowd down. That was when the sound of sleaze started to come into play. People just hung over one another, and then they would put on their sunglasses, stroll out of the club, and go for breakfast or additional acts.'" Lawrence, *Love Saves the Day*, 234.

11. The original song was written in Spanish by Mexican songwriter María Grever in 1934.

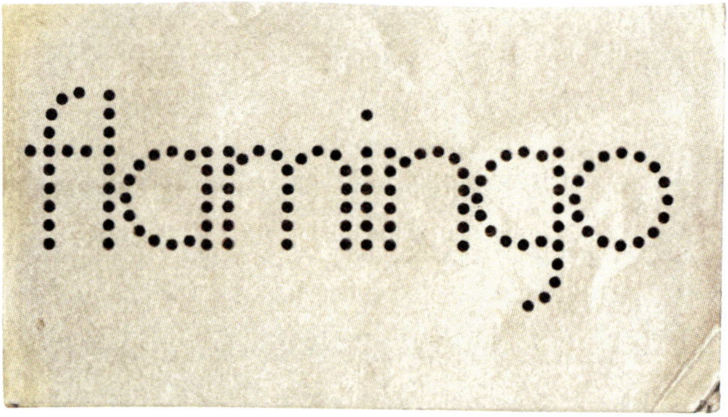

Flamingo membership card

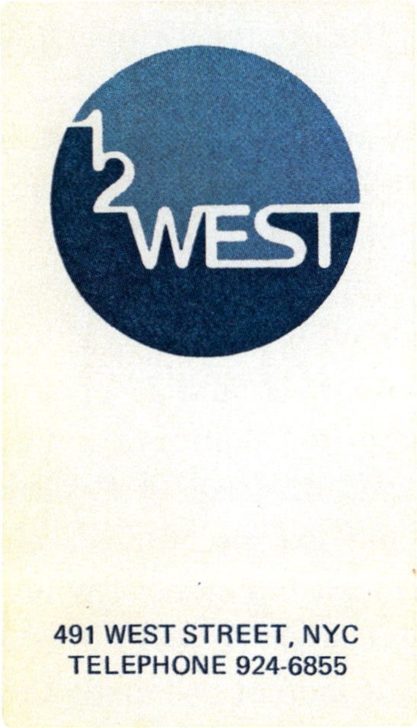

12 West membership card

physically fit body to recover from staying out all night, taking drugs, and dancing for eight hours at a stretch with rarely more than a fifteen-minute break. But by midweek, I'd be back in the swim and looking forward to the next weekend's dance party.

The Steven of the fragment is Steven Butow, who was my regular disco buddy. I don't remember for sure how or when we met, but I think it was probably through David, a mutual friend I'd picked up for sex and remained friends with until he was body-snatched by est (Erhard Seminars Training, a popular 1970s cult). Steven was part of the Baltimore crowd around John Waters (he played Lieutenant Grogan in *Desperate Living* [1977]), and we sometimes went dancing in a group that variously included Divine (in his Glenn Milstead guise), Cookie Mueller, David Lochary, and Van Smith. Steven and I occasionally slept together, but our bond was really about dancing. He worked as an illustrator for Butterick Patterns, and I was teaching at the School of Visual Arts and struggling to find my voice as a critic. We rarely saw each other during the week and had little in common beyond our disco companionship, but to that we were extremely faithful. Having a dance partner who wasn't a boyfriend worked well for disco: it kept the emotional experience musical and communal, uncomplicated by the petty jealousies that come with lovers who are just as attracted as you are to the guys dancing nearby. If Steven said, "Let's go dance next to Bobby—he's hot," I thought, Sure, let's. And

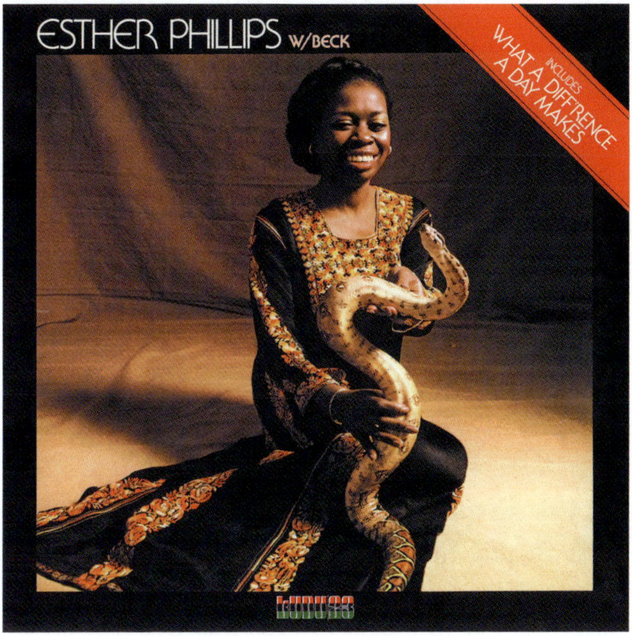

Cover of Esther Phillips's album *What a Diff'rence a Day Makes*, 1975

Steven or I could wander off and dance with whomever we pleased, knowing that we'd find our way back to each other soon enough and always be there at the end of the night to leave together. I don't think there was ever a time when either of us went home with someone else. "Dance partner" doesn't mean the same thing for disco as it does for, say, Fred and Ginger. With disco at its best, dancing is both individual and collective. You might connect with the stranger dancing next to you at a given moment, but it's not a couples thing; it's boogie intimacy, which can be very intense and sexy, but it's usually limited to dancing together for a while before you each dissolve back into the crowd or return to your "partner."

In this respect, the innovations of disco mirrored the ethos of gay liberation regarding the expansion of affectional possibility. Coupling was newly seen not as a "happily-ever-after" compact but as an in-the-moment union for sharing pleasure. Such pleasure sharing could, of course, lead to all kinds of longer-term relationships: now-and-again casual sex partners, regular fuck buddies, cruising comrades, bar and bathhouse companions, just plain friends, and combinations of any of these and many more. But it didn't have to lead to anything at all. Pleasure was its own reward; it didn't require redemption through love or commitment or even an exchange of phone numbers. Moreover, two stopped being a magic number: coupling could easily multiply to become a three-way, a foursome, group sex.

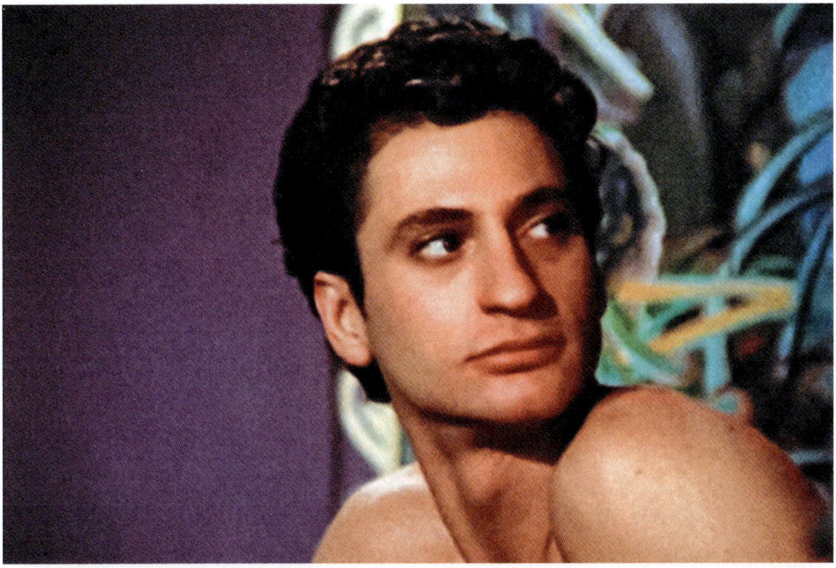

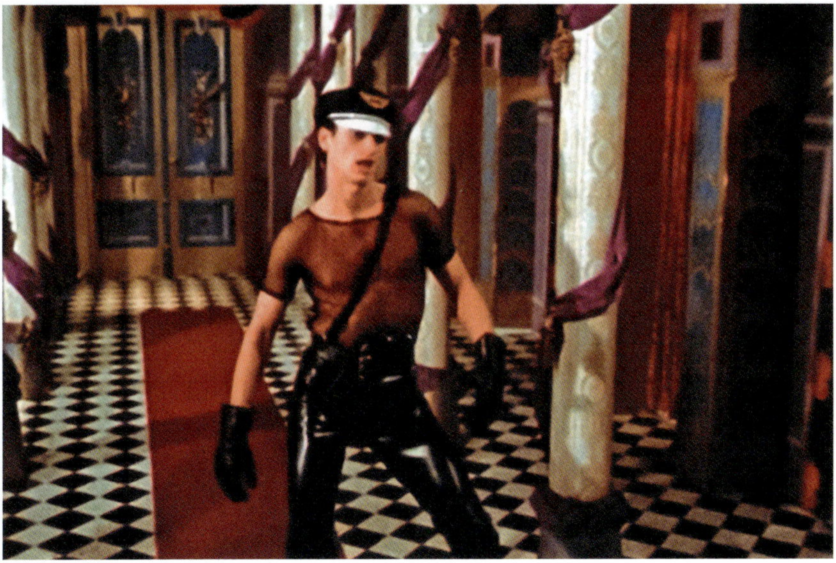

Steven Butow as Lieutenant Grogan in *Desperate Living,* 1977.
Directed by John Waters

Bathhouses had “orgy rooms,” steam rooms, and saunas for those who wanted more than one partner at a time, a little voyeurism and/or exhibitionism in the mix, or the total anonymity of sex in the dark with bodies detached from personhood. The liberation ethos developed into a new sexual culture, and that culture fed into the new dance scene. It’s not surprising that one of the earliest gay dance parties in New York happened at a bathhouse: the Continental Baths introduced disco in 1970.

I never went there. I missed out on Bette Midler’s legendary performances. I never went to the Loft or the Gallery. I never danced at the Ice Palace in Cherry Grove. I didn’t go to the Garage as often as I now wish I had. I went only once, by invitation, to Studio 54 but hated its “you-can-come-in-but-you-can’t” door policy and found it dull once I got inside. Obviously, I wasn’t there for one of the big occasions. I found the Saint exciting more as a brilliantly designed environment than as a place to dance. And the lure of the sex taking place in the balcony above the dance floor’s domed scrim confounded my notion that a truly great disco was meant to make sex redundant, at least on the night you went dancing.

I never skated at the Roxy, even though I had been early to take up roller disco. I had a crush on a French dancer, a gorgeous straight guy named Daniel, who introduced me to it. Having been a roller skater in my teens, I was game to go with him to the old Empire Rollerdrome in Crown Heights, Brooklyn, where roller disco is said to have started. We were usually the only white boys there,[12] and though good skaters, we were seriously outclassed by the regulars, who skate-danced double-time to the pounding disco music and flashing strobe lights. Sometimes they formed long chains by grabbing one another around the waist. The men were so fierce that women weren't allowed on the floor with them except during occasional "couples skates" to music with a slower beat. Otherwise it was either "women's skate" or "men's skate," with the nonskating sex hanging out in a fenced area in the middle of the rink. One fateful night skating at Empire just after Christmas in 1978, I was unintentionally clipped from behind, my legs went out from under me, and I fell—hard. I blacked out and only came to when I was on my feet again, having been scooped up by one of the floor monitors. There I was, stunned, standing in the middle of the rink with skaters zooming past me. Somehow I managed to push myself to the side of the rink with all my weight on my left leg, the only one that would support me. Although it took a while for me to admit it to myself, I'd broken my hip. By the time we called 9-1-1 and got an ambulance, I was in excruciating pain. I was taken to the medical facility nearest the Empire Rollerdrome, X-rayed, shot full of morphine, and, since I had no health insurance, sent to a ward with fifteen other guys. Within several years

12. I recently learned that during his residency at the Institute for Art and Urban Resources at PS1 in 1978, German photographer Thomas Struth also frequented the Empire Rollerdrome.

of going bankrupt and closing, Brooklyn Jewish Hospital was a pretty forlorn place. When I woke up early the next morning to the sound of boom boxes, there were cops hovering over my ward mates, most of whom were handcuffed to their bed frames while they recovered from gunshot wounds. I was unfazed: I was flying on morphine, which I guess is the only drug I've ever taken that made me feel just fine. Eventually I was transferred to Cornell Medical Center for orthopedic surgery to pin my hip. For the next six weeks, I was on crutches and, owing to an especially icy winter, more or less confined to my apartment. I spent that confinement rewriting my essay "Pictures" for *October.* It was very slow going, no doubt in part because my usual work routine was disrupted by being unable to go out to the Cock Ring at the end of the evening to reward myself with a little dancing and maybe a trick. The more serious reason was the difficulty of clarifying the inchoate ideas I'd formulated in the catalogue for *Pictures,* the modest group show I'd put together for Artists Space in 1977. For that original essay, written a year and a half earlier, I attempted to apply the linguistic and poststructuralist theory I'd been reading. The theory was new to me, and so was the artwork by the artists I selected for the show, but both the theory and the art were "about" representation and thus seemed related. For the 1979 version, I returned to the notion of postmodernism that I now realize I had come up with a few years earlier for the book proposal that shared a file folder these past forty years with my

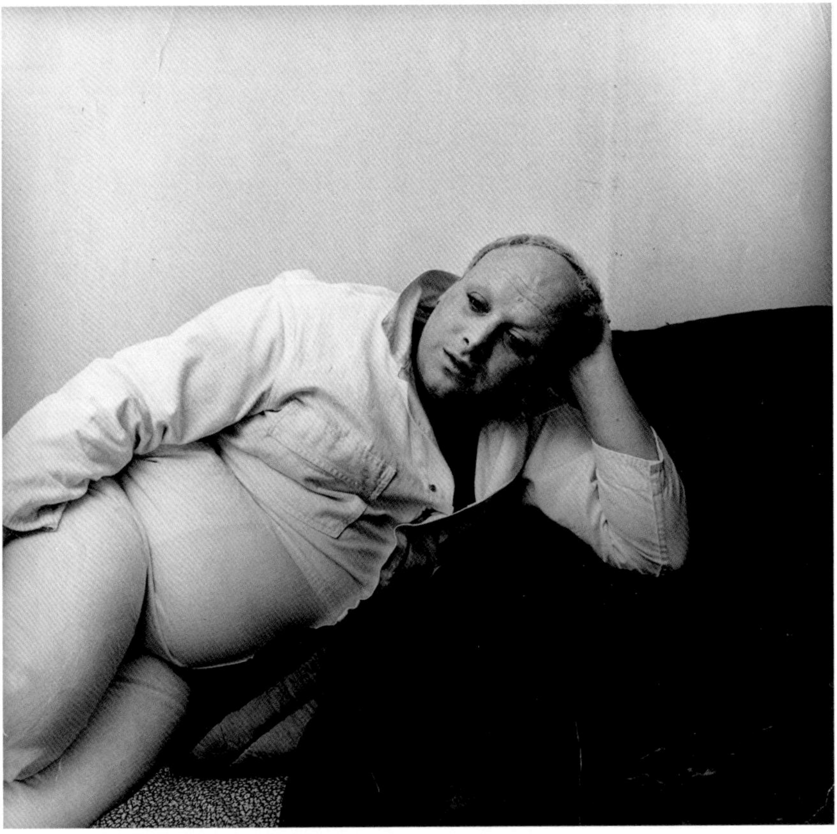

Peter Hujar, *Divine*, 1975. Gelatin silver print, 15 7⁄8 × 15 7⁄8 inches

disco fragment. This required an about-face: I concluded the 1977 essay by saying that "the self-reflexiveness and formalism of recent art appear to have been abandoned, as are interests in the specific charateristics of a medium... It would be a mistake, however, to think of this [new, Pictures] work as effecting a complete break with recent art, or with modernism as a whole."[13] The same turn away from medium specificity led me to the opposite conclusion in the 1979 version: "If postmodernism is to have theoretical value, it cannot be used merely as another chronological term; rather it must disclose the particular nature of a breach with modernism. It is in this sense that the radically new approach to mediums is important."[14] Much would be made of the shifts I made between the first essay and the second in the years to come.[15]

What did it mean that the group of young artists who came to be known as the Pictures Generation hung out at the Mudd Club? The Mudd Club opened in Tribeca in the fall of 1978, and I went there occasionally because they did—and I hated it. It was one of the principal venues of the "discosucks" backlash. The dance everyone did there was called the spastic. It's one of the only dances I could never learn to do.

13. Crimp, *Pictures*, exh. cat. (New York: Artists Space 1977), 28.

14. Crimp, "Pictures," *October*, no. 8 (Spring 1979), 87.

15. See, for example, Howard Singerman, "The Myth of Criticism in the 1980s," *X-tra 8*, no. 1 (Fall 2005), 3–16.

Lack of Information

Henrik Olesen

In 2000 I had read a report discussed in the EU parliament, that was concerned by the fact that the majority of the European Union member states did not recognise persecution for sexual orientation as a valid ground for granting asylum.[1]

As a reaction to this I collected facts regarding violence and discrimination against lesbians and gays in countries all over the world during the following year. *Lack of Information* was completed in 2001 and these pages are an excerpt from this work.

1. Recommendation 1470 (2000): Situation of gays and lesbians and their partners in respect of asylum and immigration in the member states of the Council of Europe.

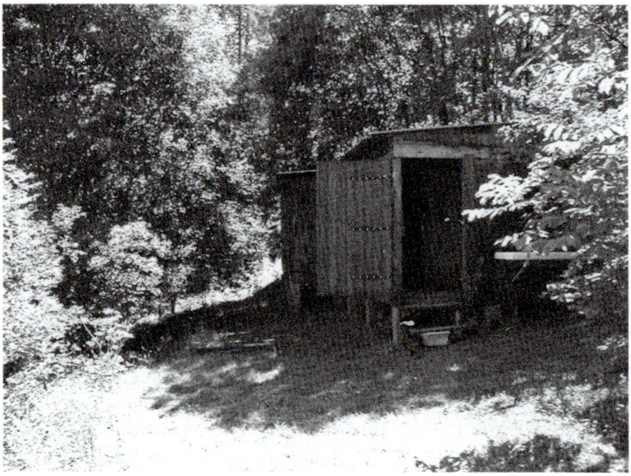

USA/Indiana (March 30, 2001)
McNaughton Park. "Park is still somewhat cruisy despite frequent patrol by local police. Several arrests have been made and names are published in local papers and local TV stations. License plate checks are a regular thing and police do harass. Most of the good hiding places have been cut down and the restrooms are locked most of the time. Dividers between doors and main part of restrooms have been removed so you have no warning if police come in."

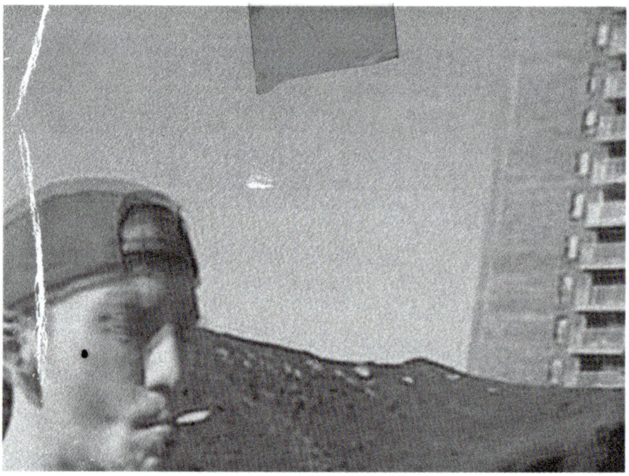

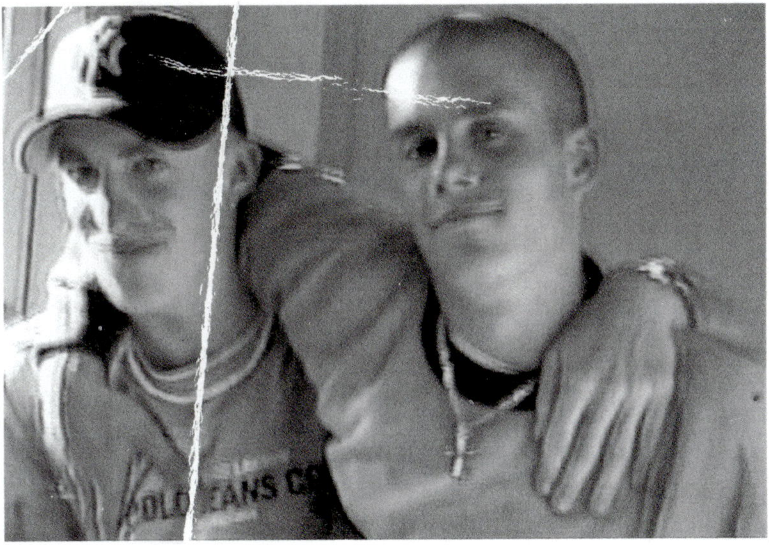

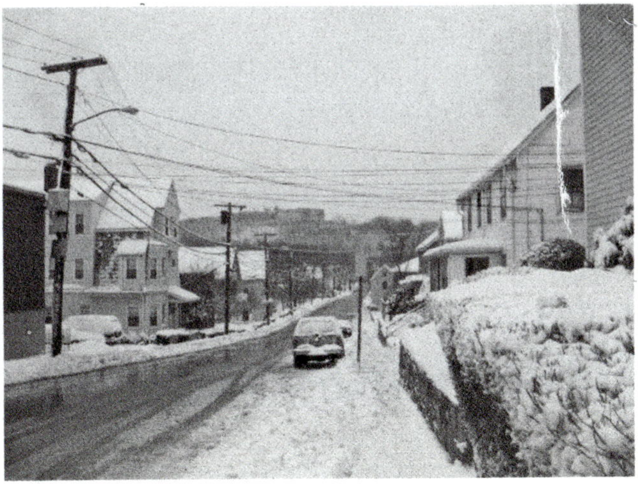

USA/Massachusetts has a sodomy law:
Maximum Penalty: 20 Years

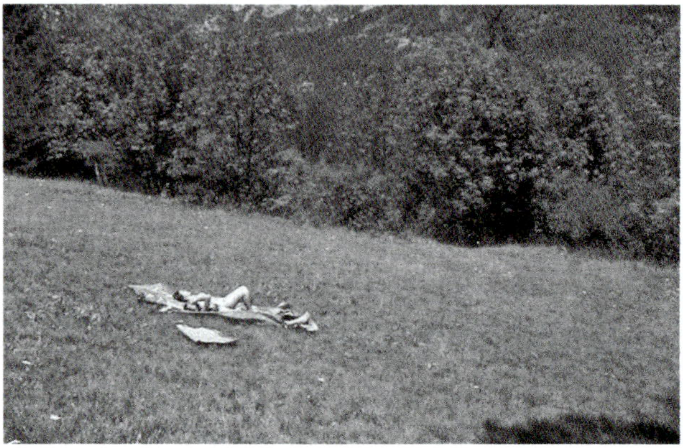

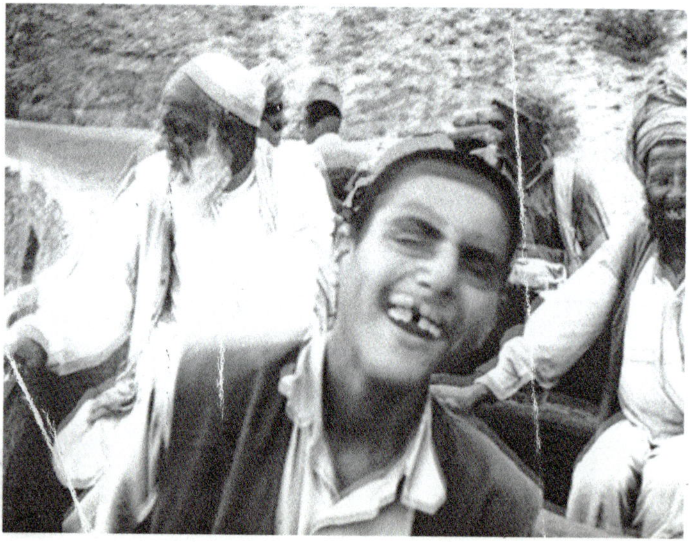

AFGHANISTAN: Homosexuality is illegal, the punishment is execution, the methods are throwing the homosexual down from a high roof or hill or by burying them beside a wall which is then toppled on to them.

Immigration/Europe:
The immigration policies in most Council of Europe member states do not recognise persecution for sexual orientation as a valid ground for granting asylum.

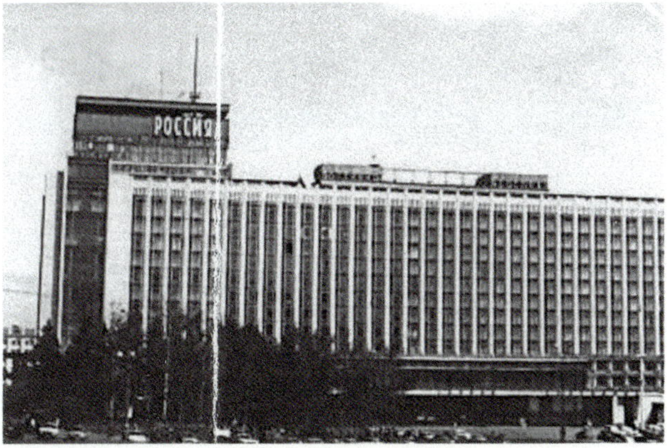

RUSSIA: Has no sodomy laws, the age of sexual consent is 14 for oral sex, and 16 for anal sex. Homosexuals are banned from the military.

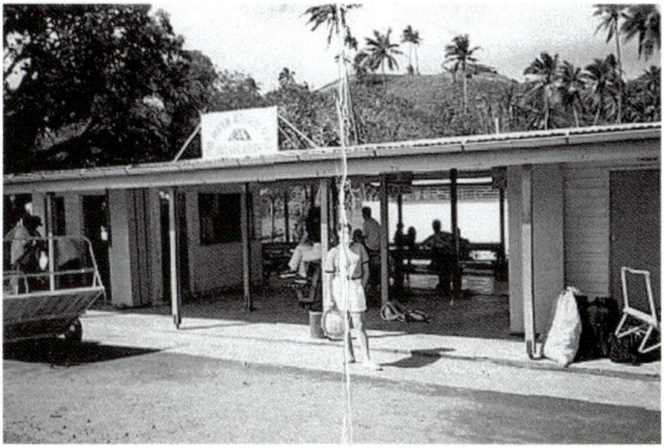

JAMAICA: Has a sodomy law, punishable with up to 10 years imprisonment and hard labour. A penalty of up to 7 years imprisonment, with or without hard labour, is provided for anyone attempting to commit homosexual acts or an "indecent assault" on another male person.

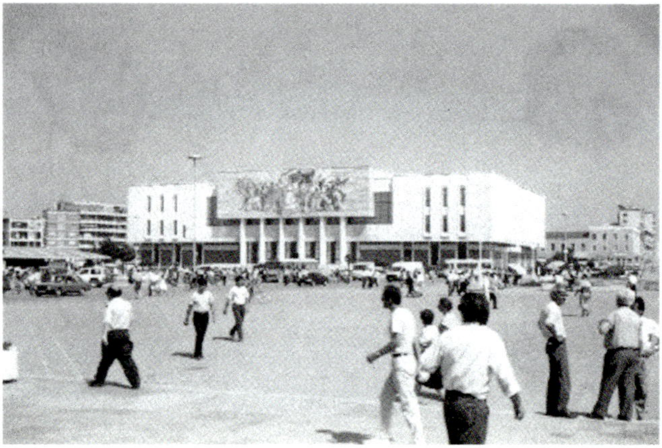

CUBA: Has no sodomy laws for private sex, but Article 303a of the Penal Code punishes "publicly manifested" homosexuality with between three months and one year in prison, or a fine of 100 to 300 cuotas for people "persistently bothering others with homosexual amorous advances".

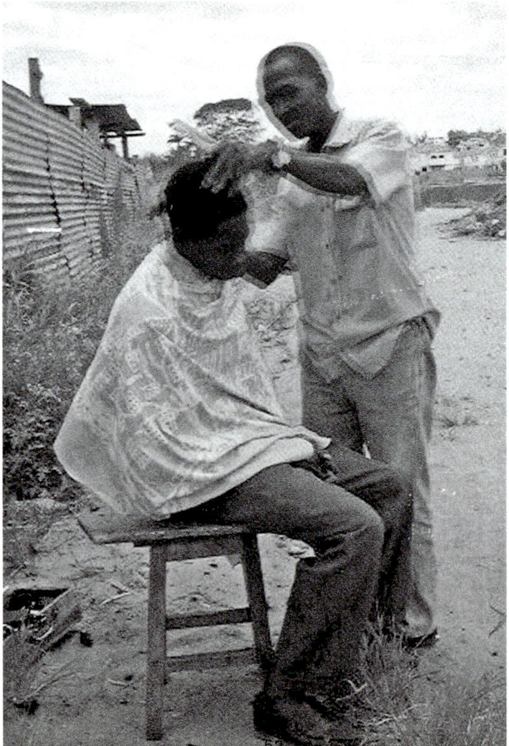

KENYA: Homosexual activity is strictly forbidden, punishable with up to 14 years in prison.

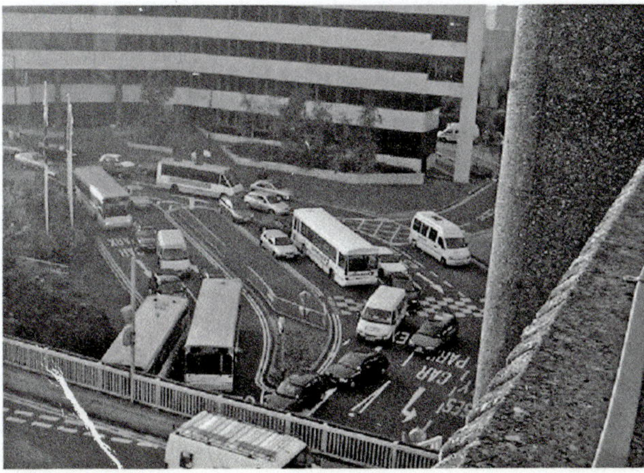

ENGLAND, SCOTLAND, WALES & NORTHERN IRELAND: Sex may only involve 2 people. Sex may only take place in ones home. Consensual S/M sex is illegal. The age of sexual consent is 18 for homosexual males, and 16 for heterosexuals and lesbians, except in Northern Ireland, there the heterosexual and lesbian age of sexual consent is 17.

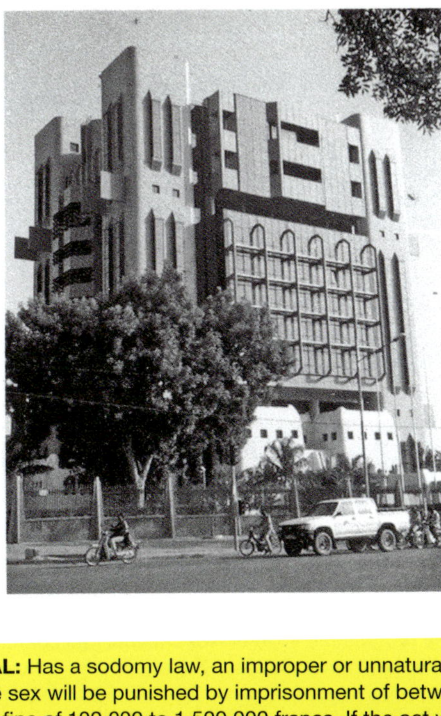

SENEGAL: Has a sodomy law, an improper or unnatural act with a person of the same sex will be punished by imprisonment of between one and five years and by a fine of 100,000 to 1,500,000 francs. If the act was committed with a person below the age of 21, the maximum penalty will always be applied.

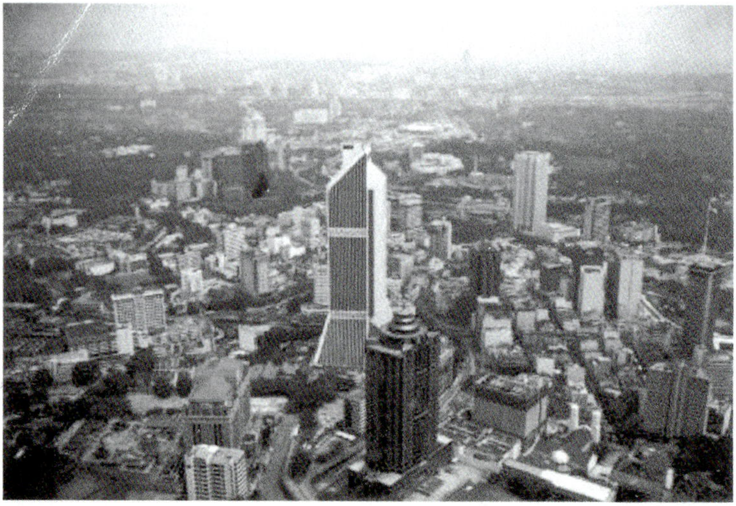

MALAYSIA: Homosexual acts are illegal, punishable by lashing and a prison sentence of up to 20 years. Cruising is illegal, punishable with up to 2 years in prison. Bans homosexuals from appearing on radio and television.

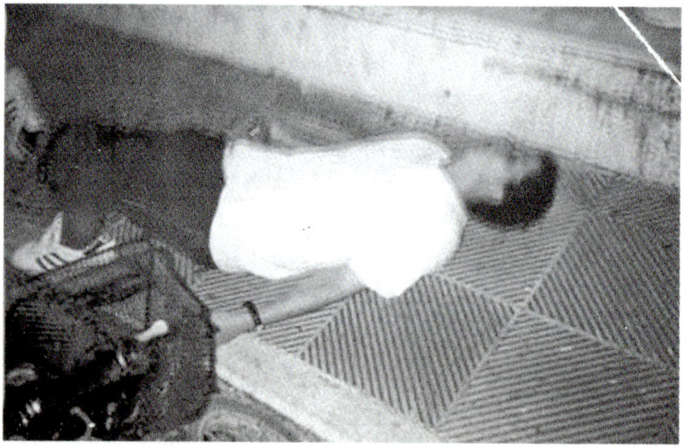

ITALY: Studies in several countries show that young lesbians and gays are between two and three times more likely to attempt suicide than their heterosexual counterparts. In Italy, in a study within the framework of the EU funded Daphne programme 40% of respondents had contemplated suicide and 13% had attempted suicide. The age in which thoughts about suicide were most prevalent was between 14 and 16, whereas the suicide attempts tended to take place in the following two years.

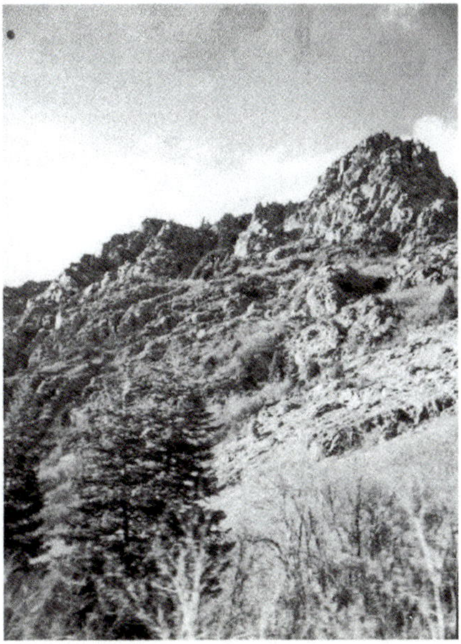

USA/Utah has a sodomy law
Maximum Penalty: 6 Months & $1,000.00 Fine.

as in Black Swans, where only males form long-term same-sex couples and rais spring, and Sage Grouse, where only females engage in group "orgies" of hom ual activity.[26] And in the majority of cases, male and female homosexualities pr their own unique blends of behaviors and characteristics that defy any simp categorization—such as Bonobos, where sexual penetration occurs in female r than male same-sex activity, where sexual interactions between adults and ad cents are a prominent feature of female interactions, and where males do not strongly bonded relationships with each other the way females do, but engage i homosexual activity overall and more affectionate activity such as openmou kissing. Once again, the diversity of animal homosexuality reveals itself down t very last detail of expression.

A Hundred and One Lesbian Acts: Calculating the Frequency of Homosexual Behavior

$$\sqrt{a} = \frac{1}{2\sqrt{E}}\left(C-\frac{D^2}{4E}\right) \qquad b=\frac{D}{2E}\left(C-\frac{D^2}{4E}\right)$$

where a, b, C, D, and E represent the number of nests with 2–6 eggs respecti

—formulas used in estimating the number o
female homosexual pairs in Gull populatic

While studying Kob antelopes in Uganda, scientists recorded exactly 101 hom ual mounts between females. In Costa Rica, 2 copulations between males we served during a study of Long-tailed Hermit Hummingbirds. In which spe homosexuality more frequent? The answer would appear to be obvious: Kob. ever, simply knowing the total number of homosexual acts observed in each s is not sufficient to evaluate the prevalence of homosexuality. For example, it be that the Kob were observed for a much longer period of time than the mingbirds, in which case the greater number of same-sex mounts would not sarily reflect any actual difference between the two species. What we really ne measure of the *rate* of homosexual activity—that is, the number of homo "acts" performed during a given period of time. To determine this, we have to

Formula as used in estimating the number of female homosexual pairs in Gull populations

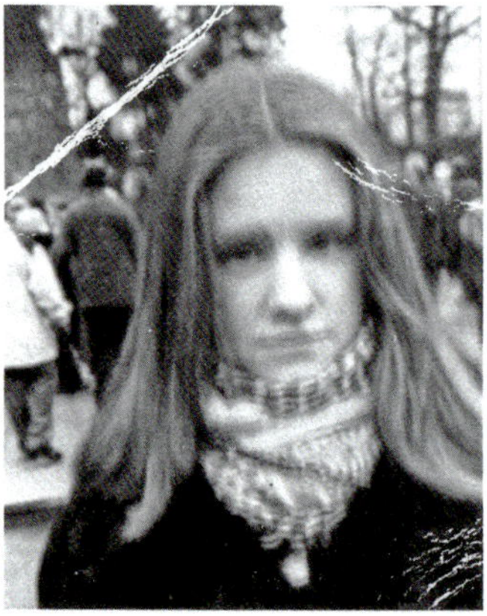

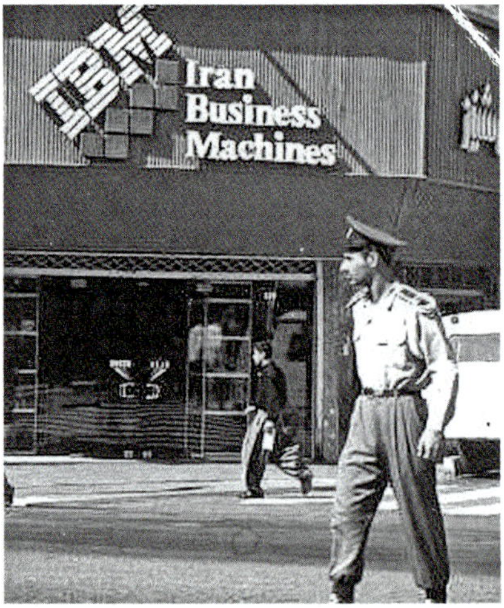

IRAN: Homosexuality is illegal, those charged with love-making are given a choice of four death styles: being hanged, stoned, halved by a sword, or dropped from the highest perch. According to Article 152, if two men not related by blood are discovered naked under one cover without good reason, both will be punished at a judge's discretion. Gay teens (Article 144) are also punished at a judge's discretion. Rubbing one's penis between the thighs without penetration (tafheed) shall be punished by 100 lashes for each offender. This act, (known to the English speaking world as "frottage") is punishable by death if the "offender" is a non-Moslem. If frottage is thrice repeated and penalty-lashes have failed to stop such repetitions, upon the fourth "offence" both men will be put to death.

Immigration/Council of Europe member states: Most countries claim not to have had to deal with an asylum request founded on sexual orientation.

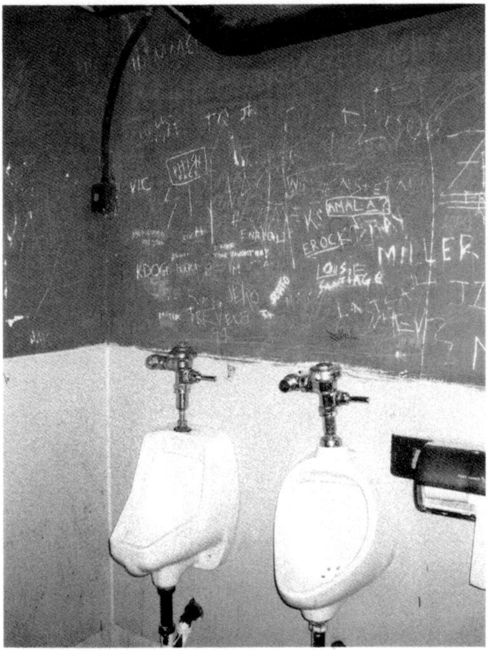
VIC
PHISH FACE
AMALA?
EROCK
MILLER
KDOG
JEKO

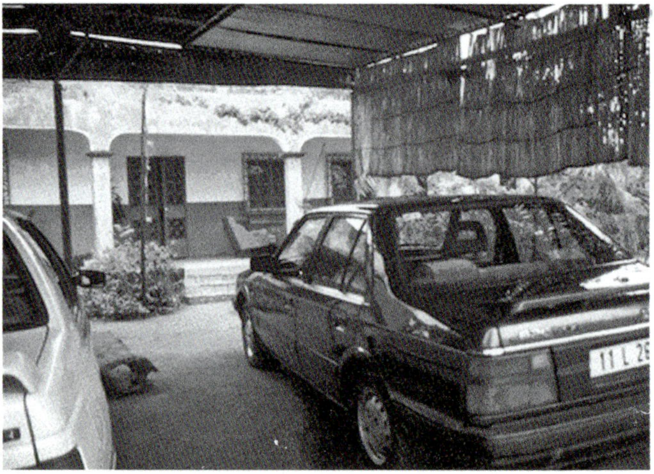

BURKINA FASO: Has no sodomy laws, the age of sexual consent is 21 for homosexuals, and 13 for heterosexual. Homosexual activity with someone under 21 is punishable with up to 3 years imprisonment.

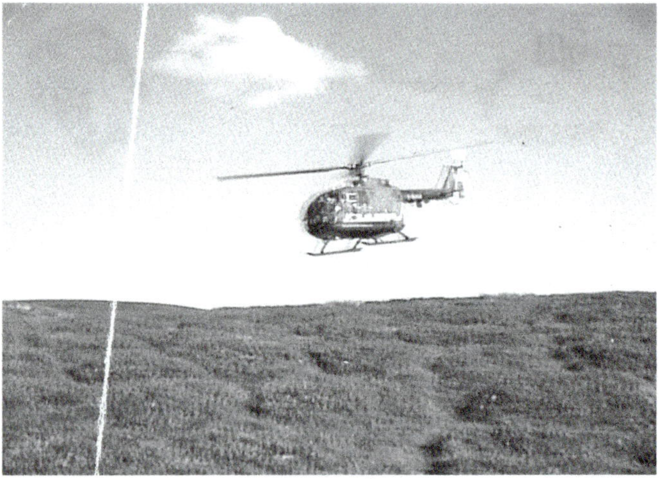

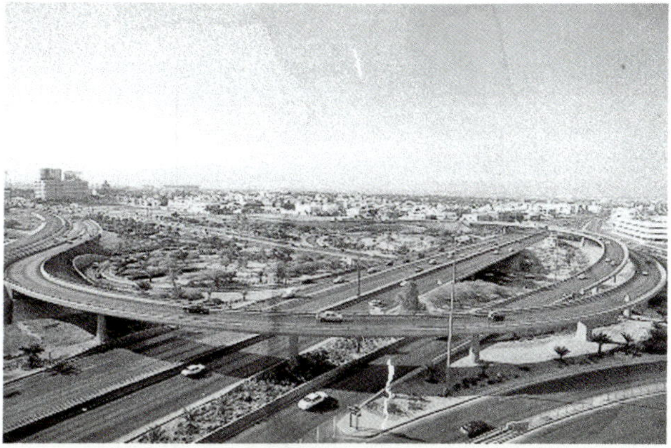

The overwhelming majority of people with HIV, some 95% of the global total, live in the developing world. That proportion is set to grow even further as infection rates continue to rise in countries where poverty, poor health systems and limited resources for prevention and care fuel the spread of the virus.
Source: UNAIDS Joint United Nations Programme on HIV/AIDS, "AIDS Epidemic Update December 2000" and "Report on the global HIV/AIDS epidemic June 2000".

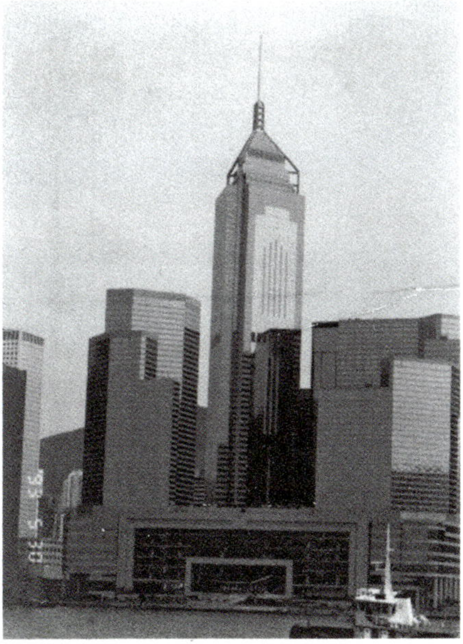

HONG KONG: Has no sodomy laws, the age of sexual consent is 21 for homosexual males, and 16 for heterosexuals and lesbians.

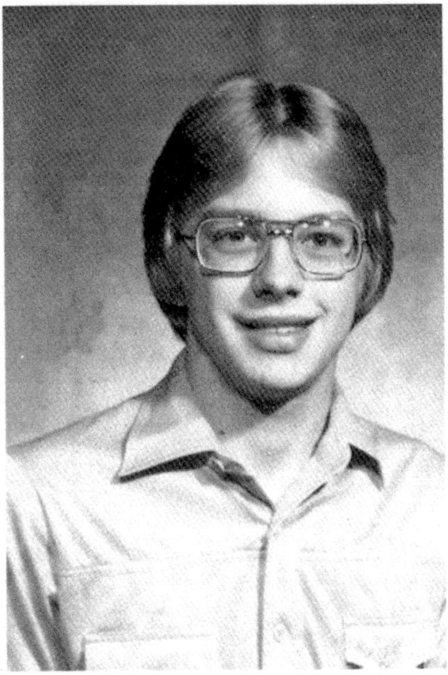

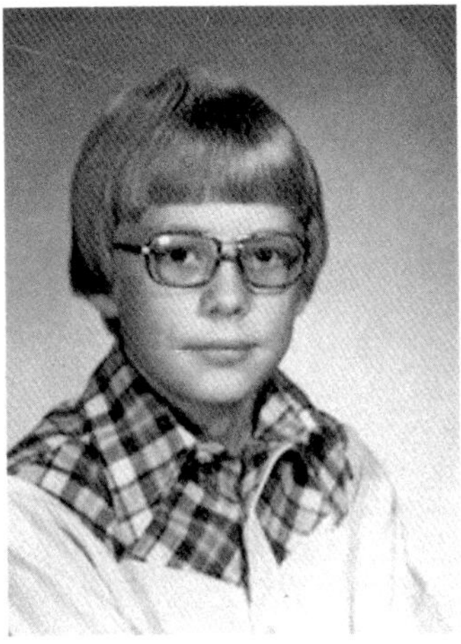

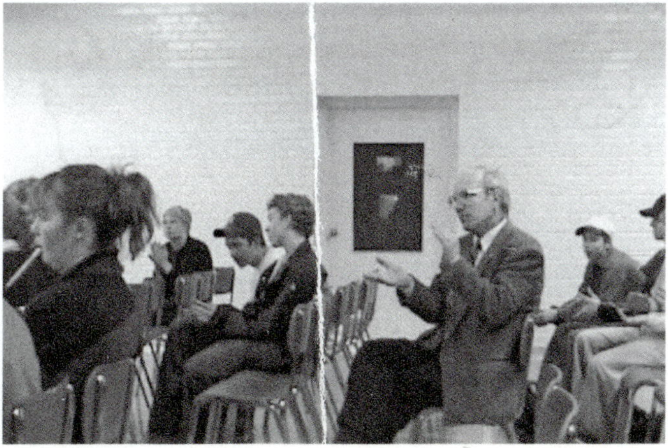

USA/Louisiana has a sodomy law
Maximum Penalty: 5 Years & $2,000.00 Fine.
The law applies to Homosexuals only.

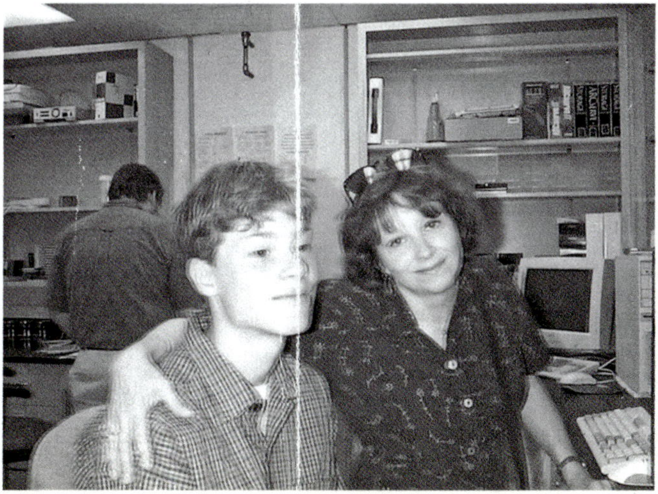

COUNTRIES THAT HAVE A HIGHER AGE OF SEXUAL CONSENT FOR HOMOSEXUALS THAN FOR HETEROSEXUALS:
Albania, Antigua and Barbuda, Australia, Austria, Bahamas, Brazil, Bulgaria, Burkina Faso, Channel Islands, Chile, Croatia, Cyprus, Ireland, Estonia, Falkland Islands/Malvinas, Faroe Islands, Gibraltar, Hong Kong, Hungary, Liechtenstein, Portugal, South Africa, Suriname, United Kingdom

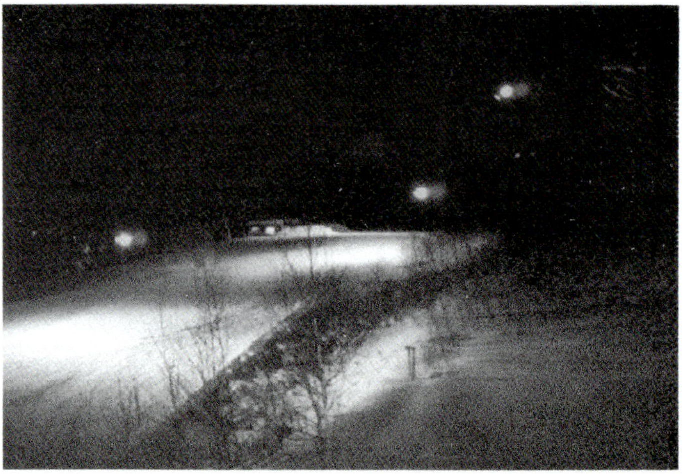

USA/Virginia (March 25, 2001)
Citywide alert. "The Washington Post on March 24 reported that police have arrested three hundred people all along the G-W Parkway from Alexandria to Arlington in a "clean-up" campaign over the last few months, citing complaints from tourists who objected to seeing sex acts at historic and scenic spots along the Parkway."

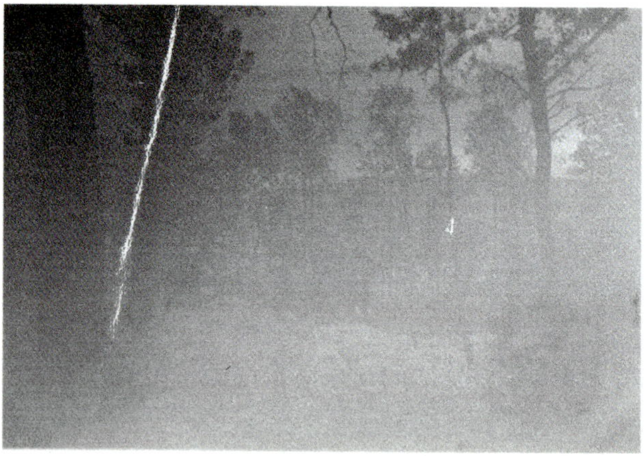

USA/Washington (October 1, 2000)
LBJ Memorial Grove. "Arrests by U.S. federal park police in parks on the Virginia side of the Potomac River and prosecutions by the U.S. Attorney for the Eastern District of Virginia continue unabated. So far, this year over 300 men have been arrested. Many have been entrapped by plainclothes officers. "

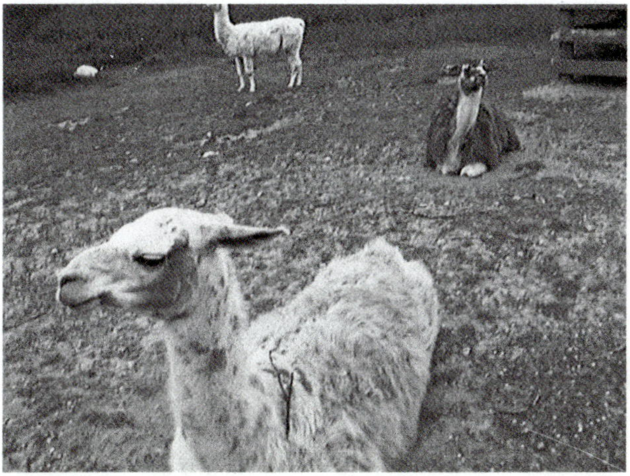

PERU: Has no sodomy law for non-military/police. In the military and police forces the performance of "dishonourable acts of carnal knowledge against the order of nature" with a person of the same sex can be punished with 60 days to 20 years imprisonment, in some cases with discharge from the forces.

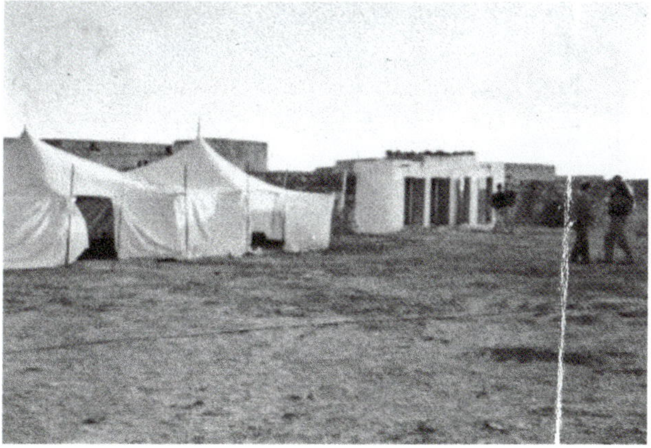

UNITED ARAB EMIRATES: Has some sodomy laws, the Abu Zhabi Penal Code makes sodomy punishable with imprisonment of up to 14 years, the Penal Code of Dubai imposes imprisonment of up to 10 years on consensual sodomy.

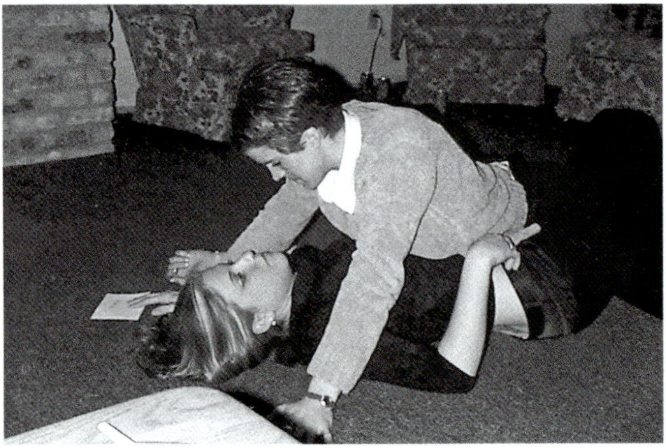

Reproductive rights: Access to medical facilities for artificial insemination is possible in Hungary only for heterosexual couples whether married or unmarried, in Slovenia for a married woman, and in Sweden for a married or cohabiting woman. In France, such access is expressly restricted to couples consisting of a man and a woman who are married or can prove that they have lived together for at least two years.

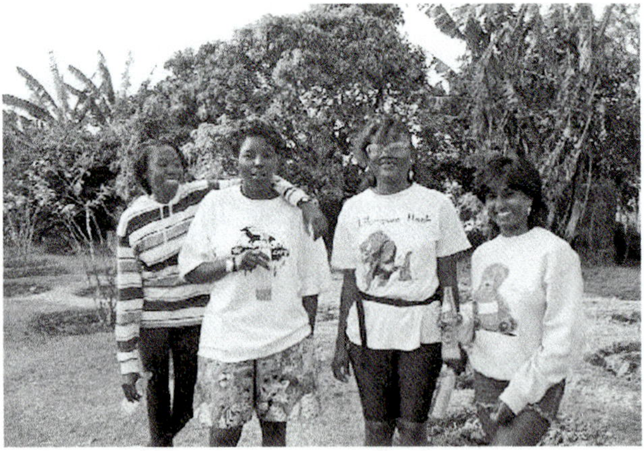

ZAMBIA has a sodomy law, punishable with 14 years imprisonment.

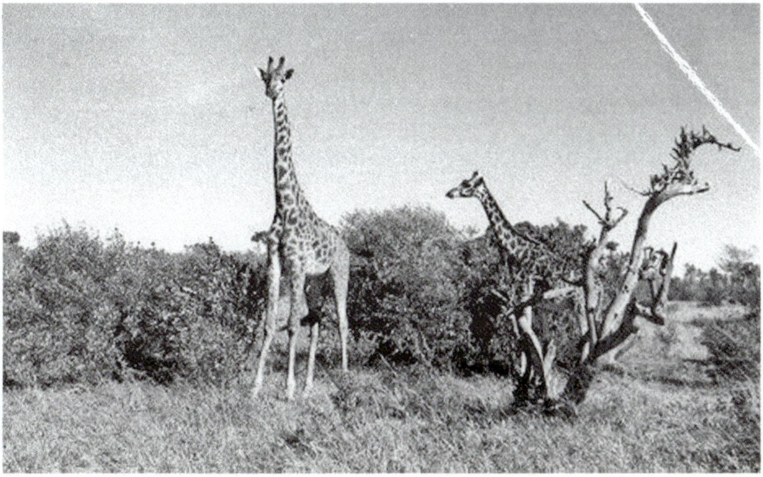

Homosexual activity is common in Giraffes and in many cases is actually more frequent than heterosexual behaviour: In one study area, mountings between males accounted for 94 percent of all observed sexual activity. Anywhere from a third to three-quarters of all courtship sessions are homosexual (i.e. they involve necking between two males), and at any given time, about 5 percent of all males are participating in necking. Among females, less than 1 percent of interactions involving body contact consist of homosexual mounting.

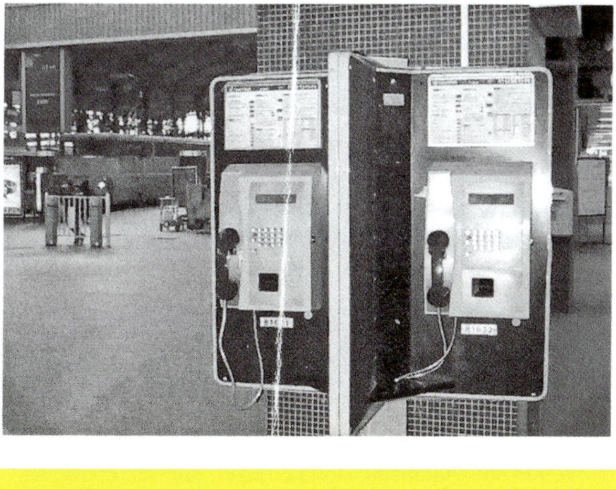

Adoption: Homosexual couples are not allowed to adopt children in Andorra, Belgium, the Czech Republic, Finland, France, Hungary, Malta, Poland, Romania, Sweden, Switzerland, etc.; only married couples are allowed to do so. In most European countries, where one member of a homosexual couple has a child the partner has no right to recognition of his/her relationship with the child. This causes problems, for instance in dealings with the school and the doctor.

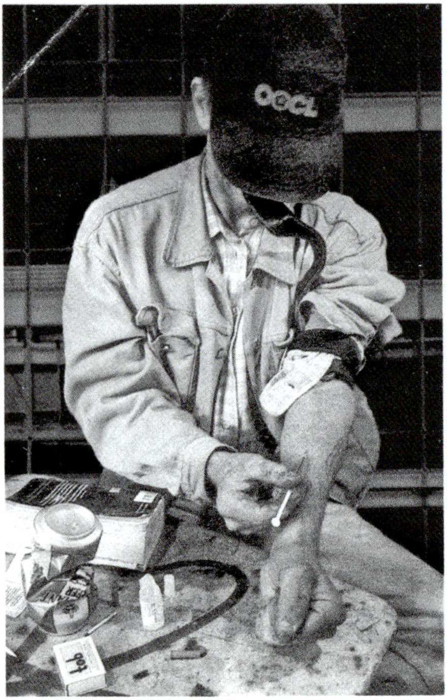

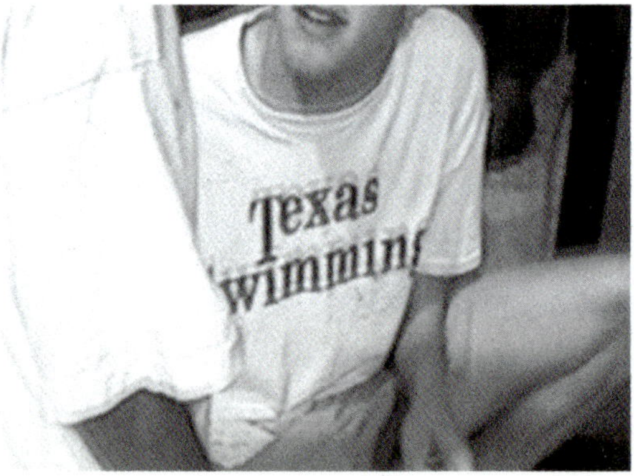

USA/STATES WITH SODOMY LAWS
Alabama, Arizona, Arkansas, Florida, Idaho, Kansas, Louisiana, Maryland, Massachusetts, Michigan, Minnesota, Mississippi, Missouri, North Carolina, Oklahoma, South Carolina, Texas, Utah, Virginia.

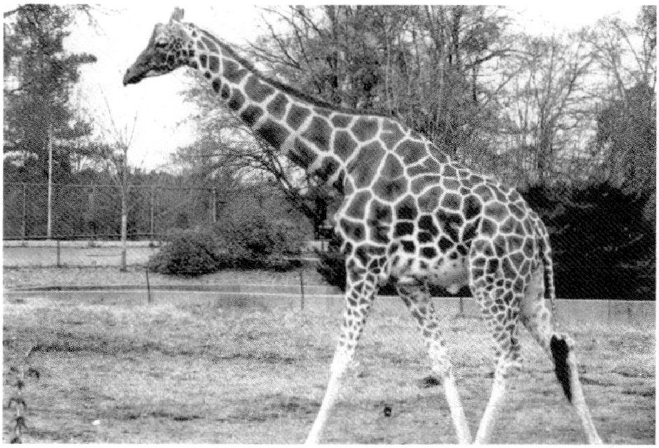

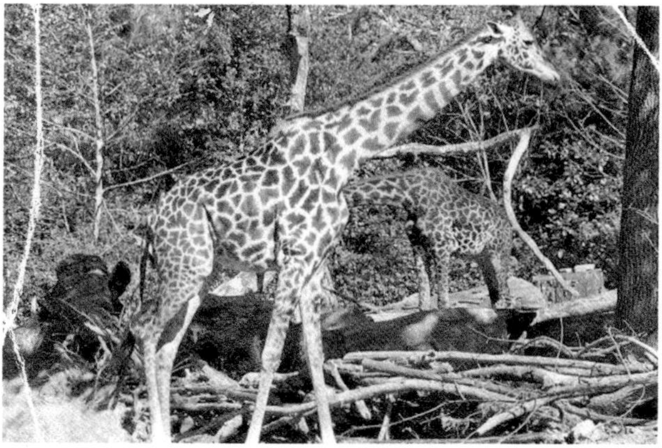

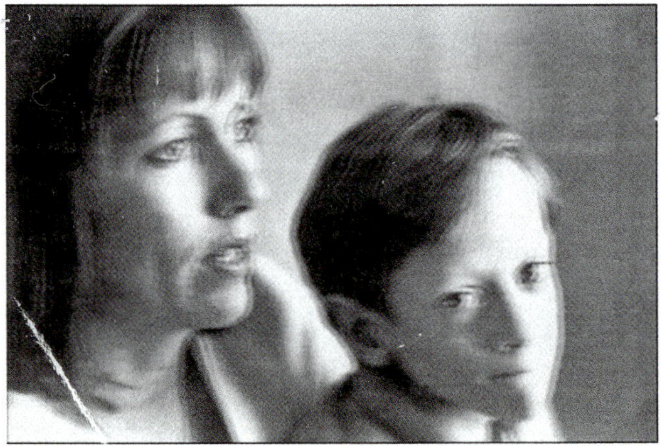

AUSTRIA: The 1992 Reproductive Medicine Act explicitly excludes lesbians and all single women from the benefit of artificial insemination or in-vitro fertilisation methods, those are restricted to married women or women in long-term heterosexual partnerships only.

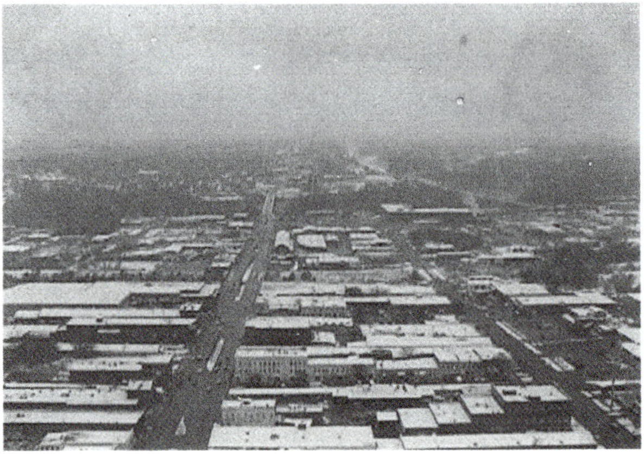

USA/South Carolina has a sodomy law: Maximum Penalty: 5 Years & $500.00 Fine.

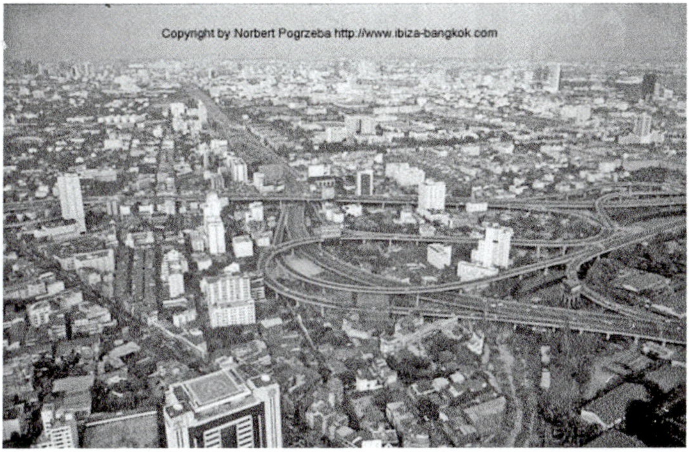

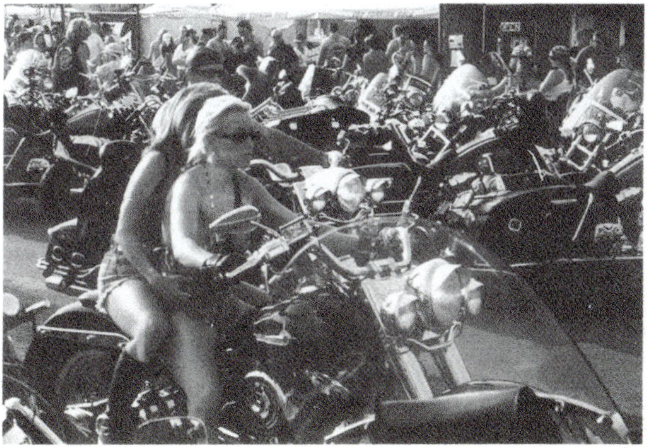

Reproductive rights: In Finland, the Netherlands and the United Kingdom, a woman living either singly or as another woman's partner can gain access to medical facilities for artificial insemination.

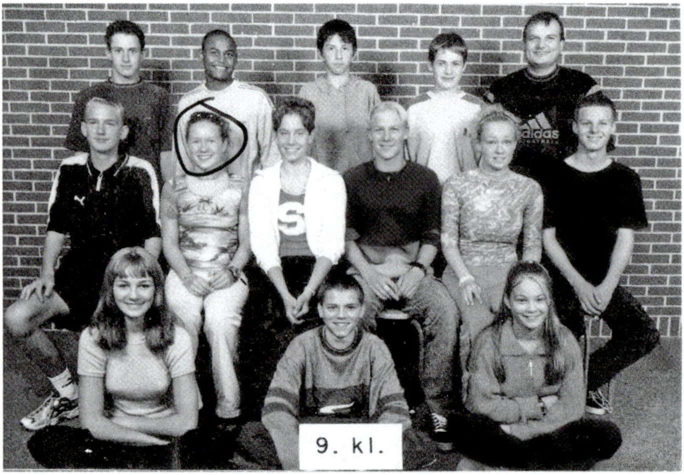

Reproductive rights: DENMARK bans assisted insemination for lesbians.

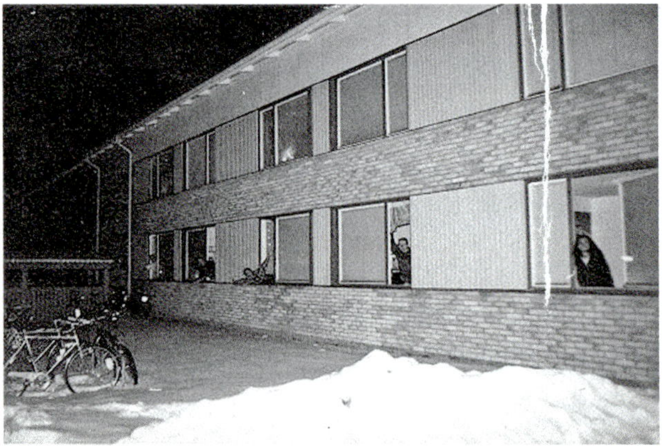

SWEDEN bans homosexuals adopting children or having children through alternative insemination.

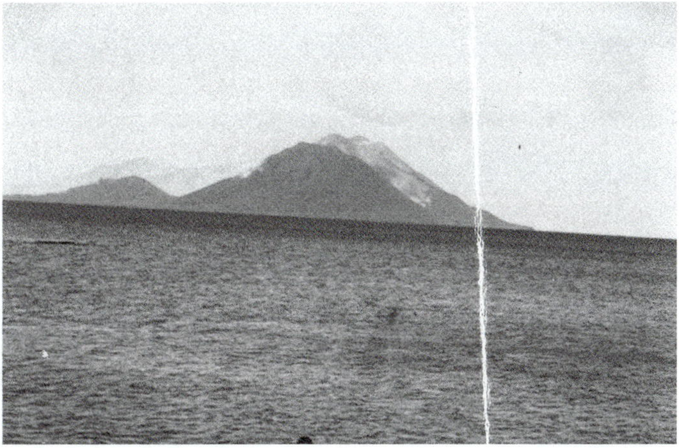

PAPUA NEW GUINEA has a sodomy law, anal intercourse is punishable with imprisonment of up to 14 years, other homosexual relations between men are punishable with up to five years imprisonment. Lesbian relations are not criminal, the age of sexual consent is 16.

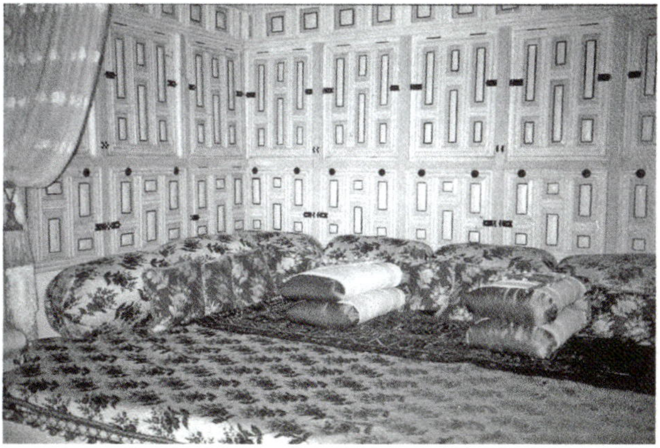

SAUDI ARABIA has a sodomy law, homosexual acts are subject to a maximum penalty of death.

Situation of gays and lesbians and their partners in respect to asylum and immigration in the member states of the Council of Europe
The immigration policies in most Council of Europe member states do not recognise persecution for sexual orientation as a valid ground for granting asylum.

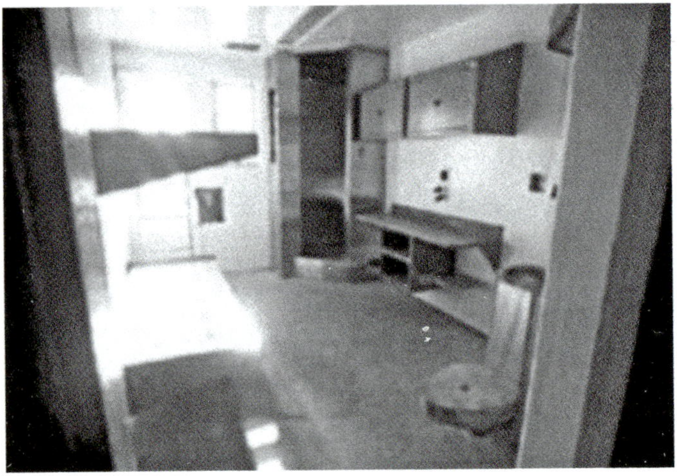

COUNTRIES WITH SODOMY LAWS (HOMOSEXUAL ACTIVITY IS ILLEGAL):
Afghanistan, Algeria, Angola, Anguilla, Armenia, Azerbaijan, Bangladesh, Barbados, Bahrain, Benin, Bhutan, Bosnia & Herzegovina, Botswana, British Virgin Islands, Brunei, Burma (Myanmar), Burundi, Cameroon, Cape Verde, Cayman Islands, Cook Islands, Djibouti, Ethiopia, Fiji, etc.

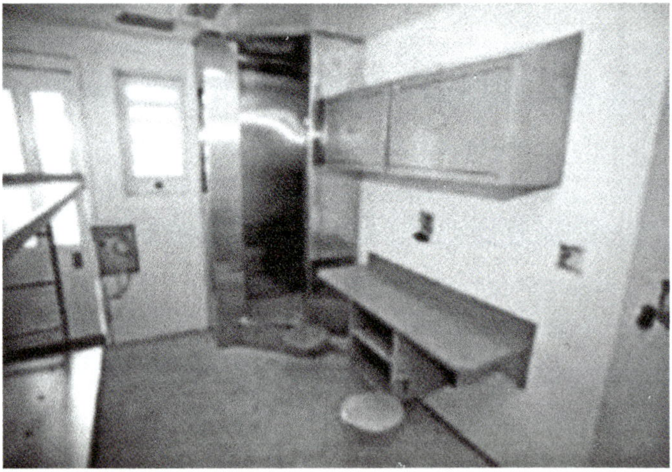

COUNTRIES WITH SODOMY LAWS (HOMOSEXUAL ACTIVITY IS ILLEGAL):
Georgia, Ghana, Grenada, Guyana, India, Iran, Jamaica, Kenya, Kiribati, Kuwait, Lebanon, Liberia, Libya, Malawi, Malaysia, Maldives, Mali, Marshall Islands, Mauritania, Mauritius, Moldavia, Montserrat, Morocco, Mozambique, Namibia, Nauru, Nicaragua, Nigeria, Niue, Oman, etc.

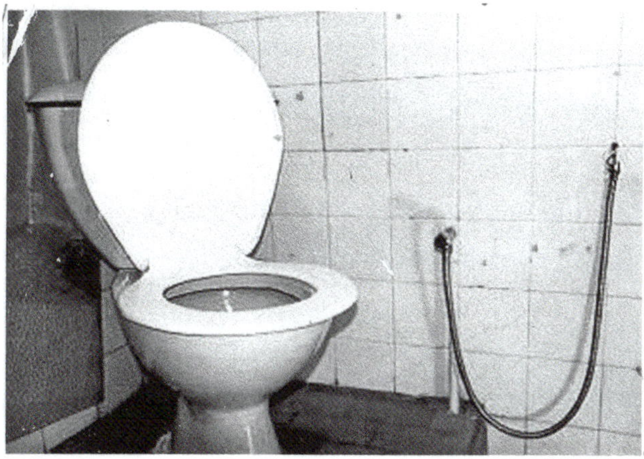

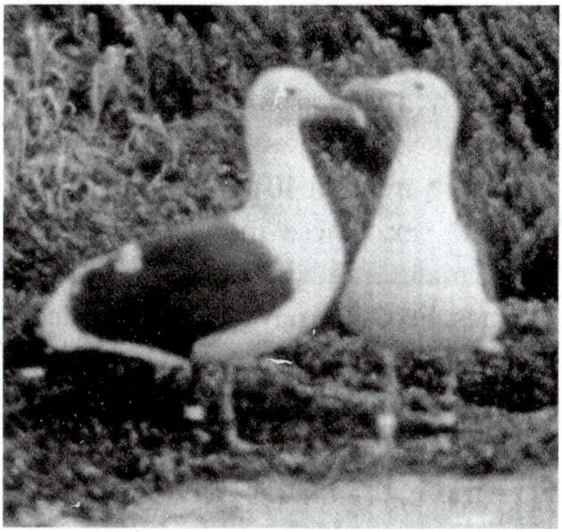

A homosexual pair of female Western Gulls in California.
Frequency of homosexual behaviour among Gulls: Ringbilled Gull: 6-12% - Western Gull: 10-15% - Silver Gulls: 12% - Herring Gulls: 3% - Black Headed Gull: 16-18%

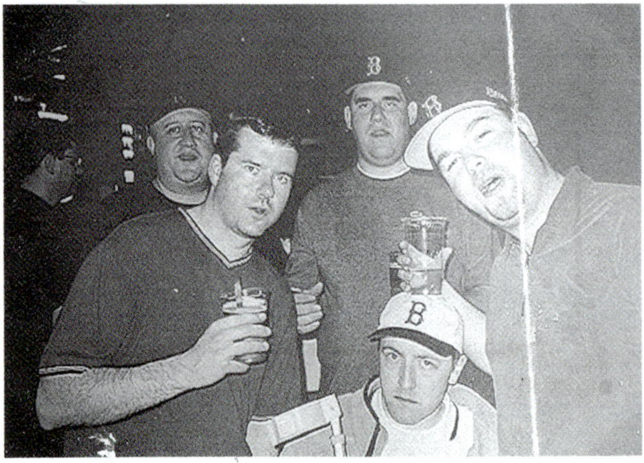

AUSTRALIA: State/Territory Age of Sexual Consent: New South Wales: 18. South Australia: 17. Northern Territory: 18. Tasmania: 17. Australian Capital Territory: 16. Victoria: 16. Queensland: 16 for oral sex & 18 for anal sex. Western Australia: 21 for gay men & 16 for lesbians. The heterosexual age of sexual consent is 16 in all but 2 states, in Tasmania and South Australia it is 17. Queensland, Northern Territory, South Australia, Victoria, and Western Australia ban donor insemination services to lesbians. Queensland bans gays and lesbians from foster parenting.

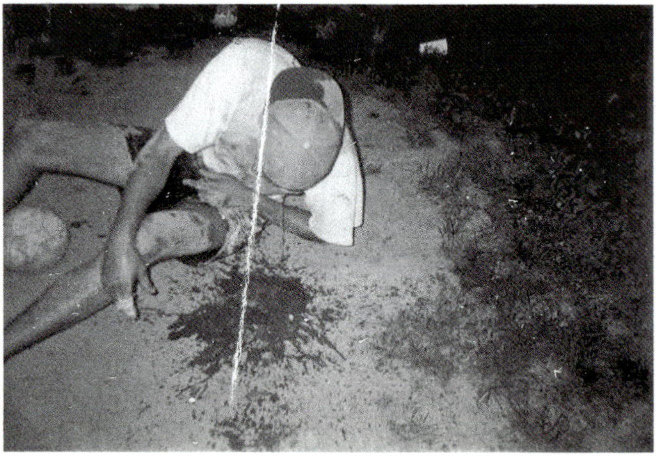

Homophobic hate crimes: In Sweden a 1996 survey dealing with homophobic hate crime against lesbian and gay men showed that 23% of the 600 lesbian and gay respondents had been victims of violent hate crime, and 40% of the sample reported that they were often in fear of hate crimes.

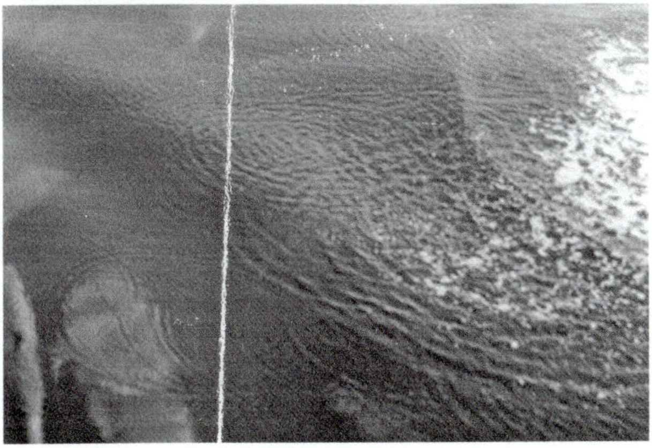

CYPRUS has no sodomy laws, the age of sexual consent is 18 for homosexuals and 16 for lesbians and heterosexuals.

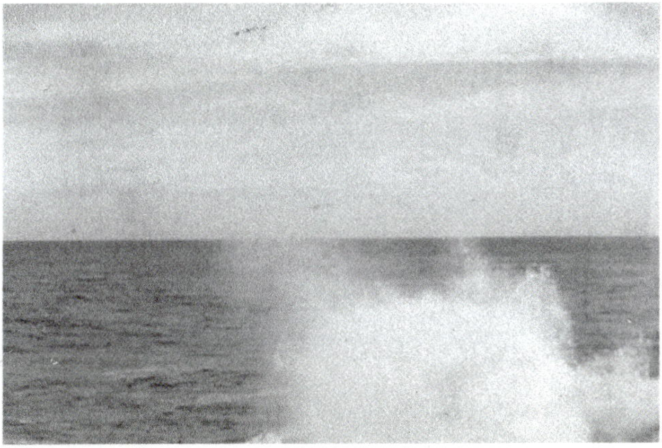

UNITED KINGDOM: DEPENDENT TERRITORY LAWS: The British Virgin Islands, Turks and Caicos Islands, Anguilla, Montserrat and Cayman Islands, all British dependent territories, have sodomy laws. The Turks and Caicos Islands Has a sodomy law for males, punishable with up to life imprisonment at the discretion of the judge. The law is silent with regard to the legal status of sexual acts between women. Gibraltar, has no sodomy laws, the age of sexual consent is 18 for homosexuals, and 16 for heterosexuals.

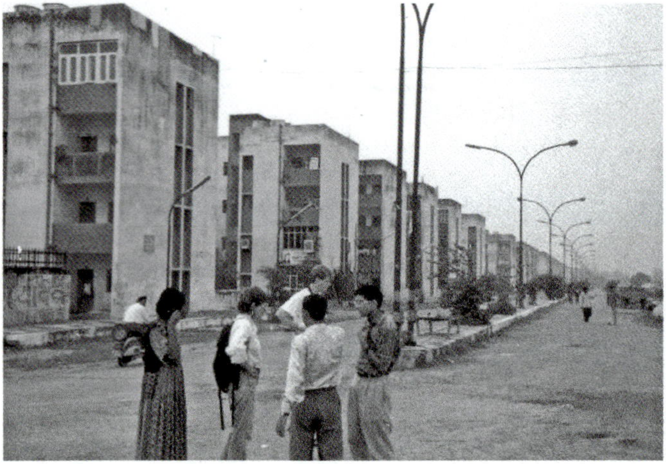

INDIA: Male homosexual sex is forbidden by law, punishable with a maximum sentence of life in prison.

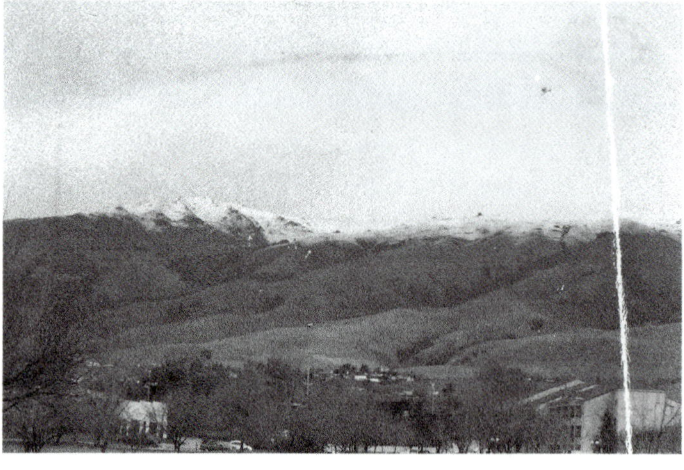

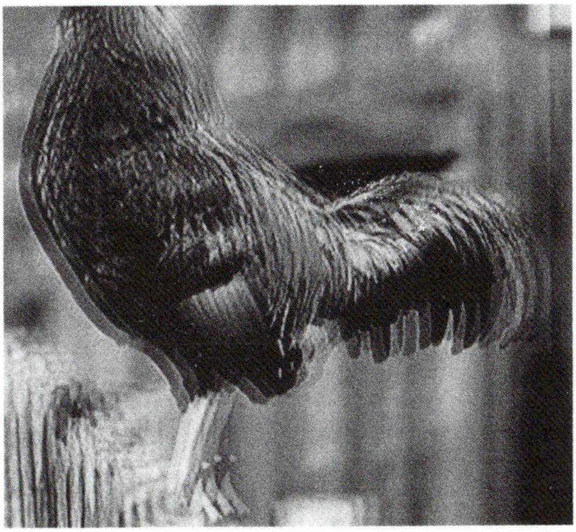

USA/Mississippi has a sodomy law:
Maximum Penalty: 10 Years.

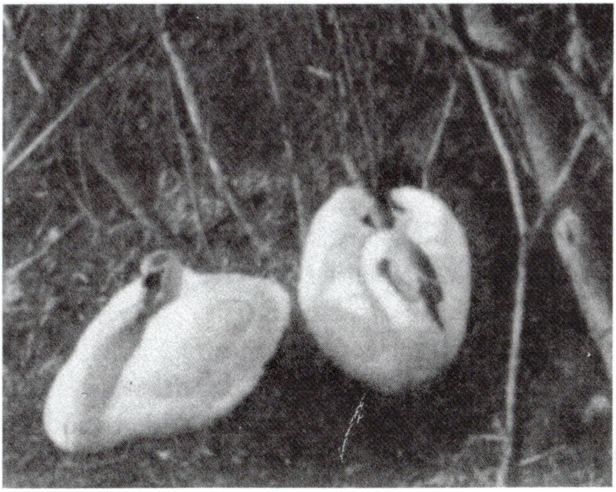

The earliest photographic record of animal homosexuality: a pair of male Mute Swans photographed in 1923 in the nest they build together in Scotland. A female pair of the same species was first observed in 1885.

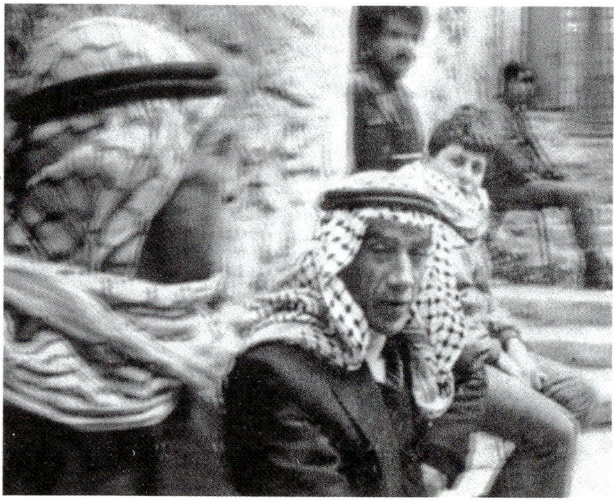

ISRAEL: Homosexual activity is legal, the age of consent is 16 for all. Allows homosexuals in its military.

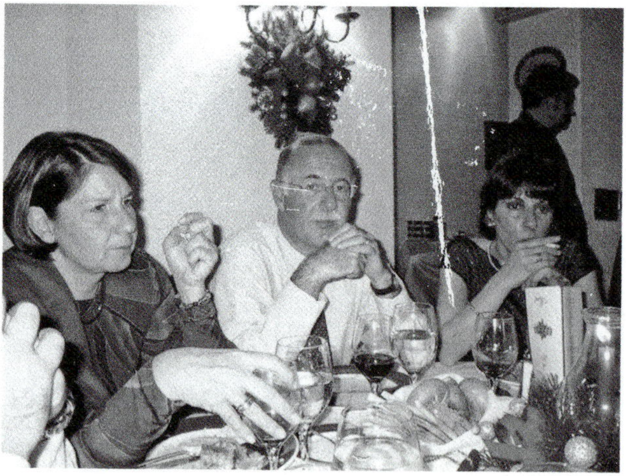

FRANCE bans artificial insemination for lesbians.

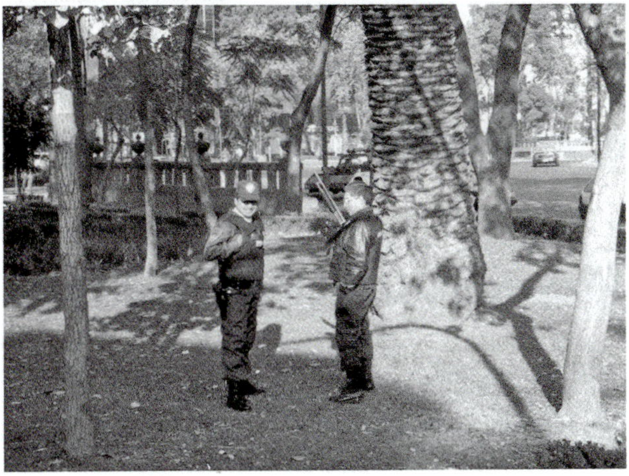

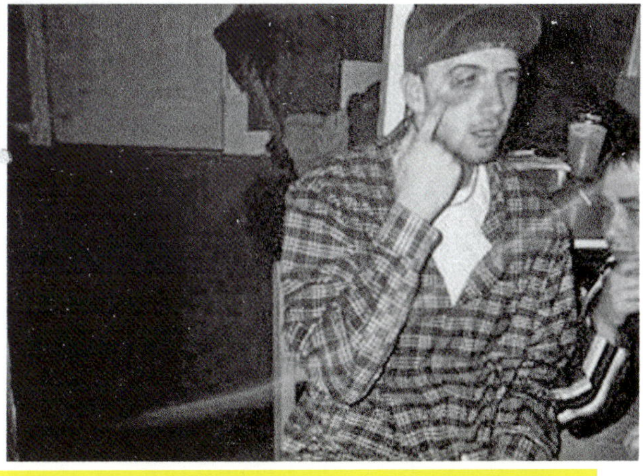

Homophobic hate crimes: In Ireland, a 1995 government-sponsored survey dealing with homophobic hate crime against lesbian and gay men found that a quarter of the 159 respondents had been punched, beaten, hit or kicked.

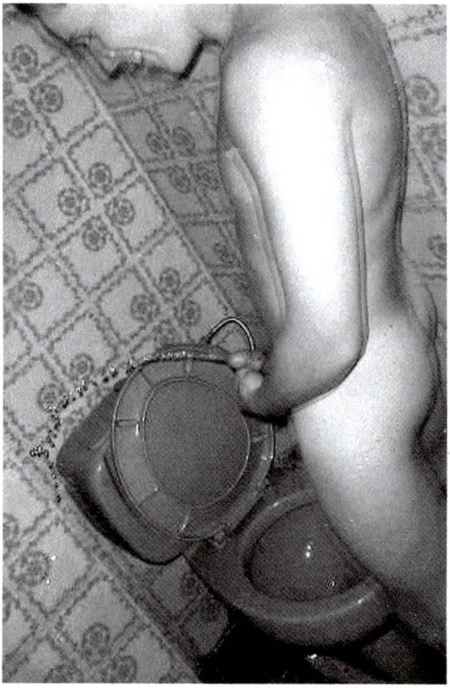

USA/Virginia has a sodomy law. Maximum Penalty: 20 Years.
Sodomy law applies to Homosexuals only.

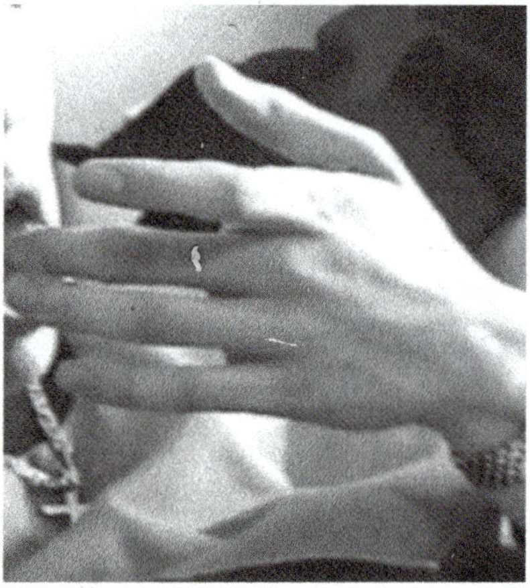

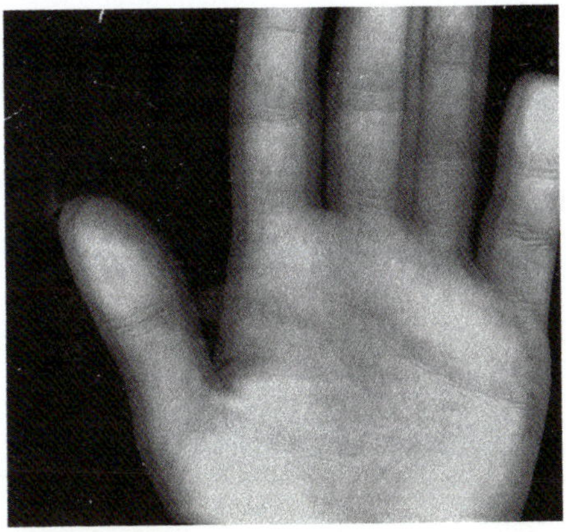

PAKISTAN: Homosexual activity is illegal, punishable with life in prison, and corporal punishment of 100 lashes, while Islamic law, which also can be enforced legally, calls for up to 100 lashes or death by stoning.

Situation of gays and lesbians and their partners in respect to asylum and immigration in the member states of the Council of Europe: The immigration policies in most Council of Europe member states do not recognise persecution for sexual orientation as a valid ground for granting asylum, and the rules concerning family reunion and social benefits usually do not apply to same-sex partnerships.

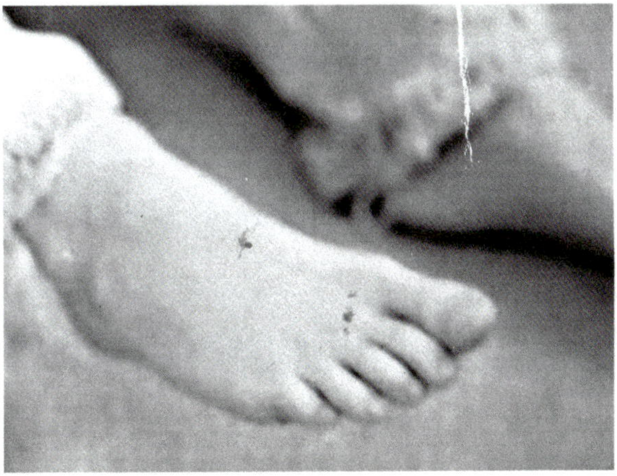

YEMEN: Homosexual activity is forbidden, punishable by death.

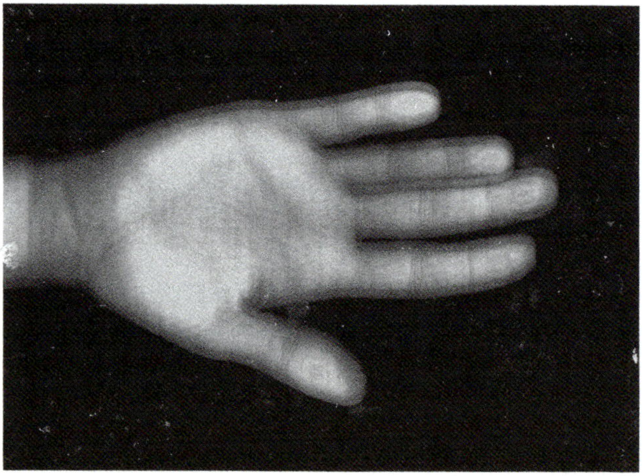

SUDAN: Homosexual activity is illegal, punishable by 100 lashes or death.

Asylum practice in Council of Europe member states: Several Council of Europe member states (Austria, Belgium, Denmark, Finland, Germany, Greece, Ireland, Latvia, the Netherlands, Norway, Sweden, U.K.) recognise in their asylum law or practice that lesbians and gay men constitute "members of a particular social group", in the wording of the 1951 United Nations Convention relating to the Status of Refugees, or have granted asylum to lesbians and gay men on "humanitarian grounds".
A lack of documentation on persecution of homosexuals by mainstream human rights groups and a general mistrust by the courts of information produced by gay and lesbian organisations makes it relatively difficult for homosexuals to produce reliable evidence of persecution.

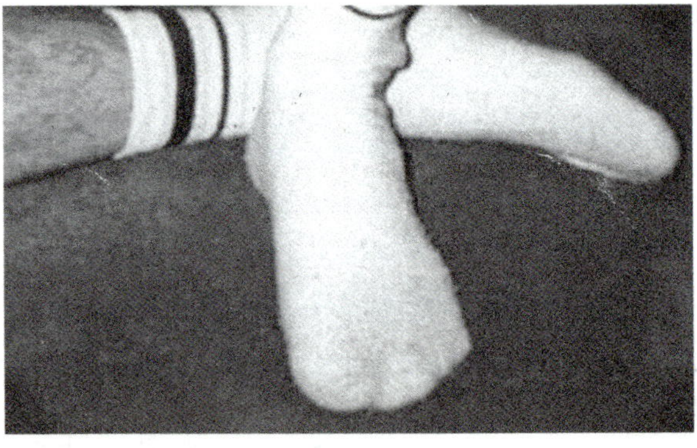

MOROCCO: Homosexual activity is illegal, which provides a penalty of between 6 months and 3 years imprisonment and additional fines from 120 to 1200 dirhams for "lewd or unnatural acts with an individual of the same sex".

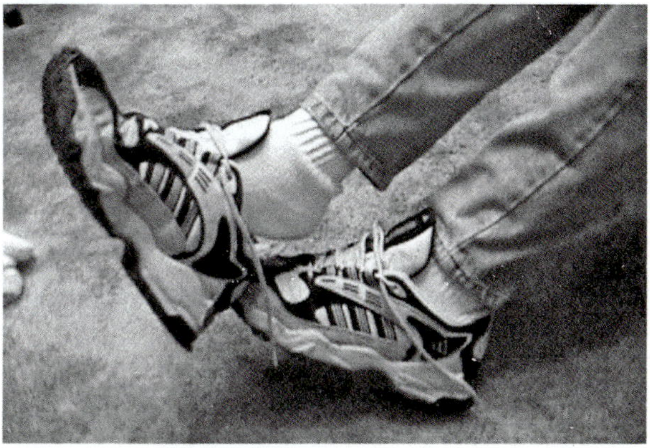

BULGARIA: In Bulgaria, same-sex sexual acts are unlawful and punishable by up to two years' imprisonment or by corrective labour in the event of scandal, of one person inciting another or if a person under 16 is involved. Homosexual men are submitted to a medical test for hepatitis B.

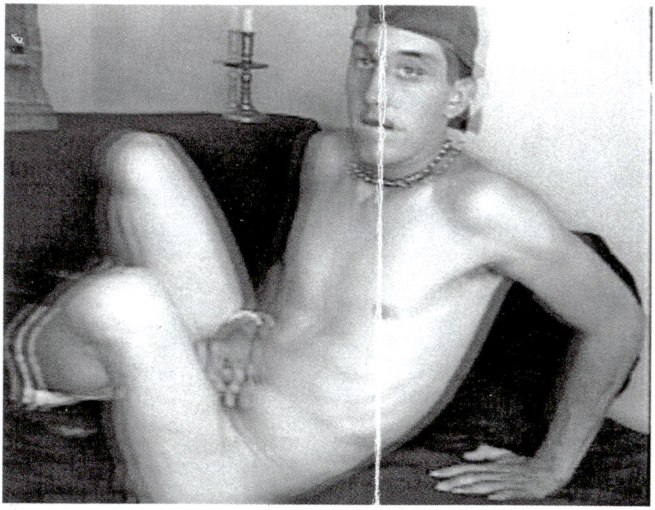

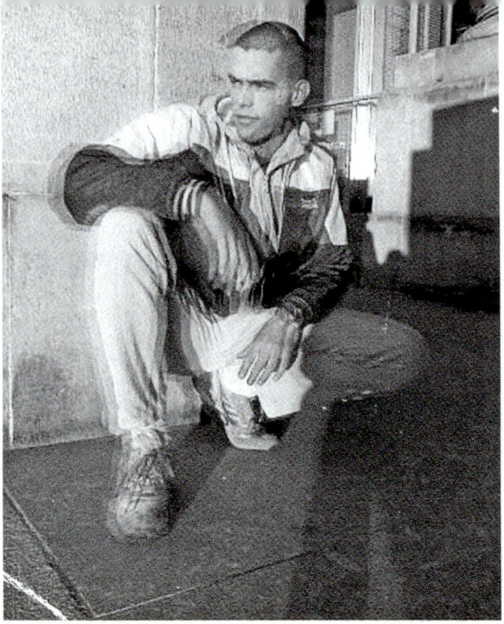

AUSTRIA: Has no sodomy laws, the age of sexual consent is 18 for gay men and 14 for lesbians and heterosexuals. "Same Sex Lewdness" with persons under 18 Years: a man over 19 years of age who engages in same-sex lewdness with a person who has attained the age of 14 but not yet the age of 18 years can be punished with imprisonment from six months to five years.

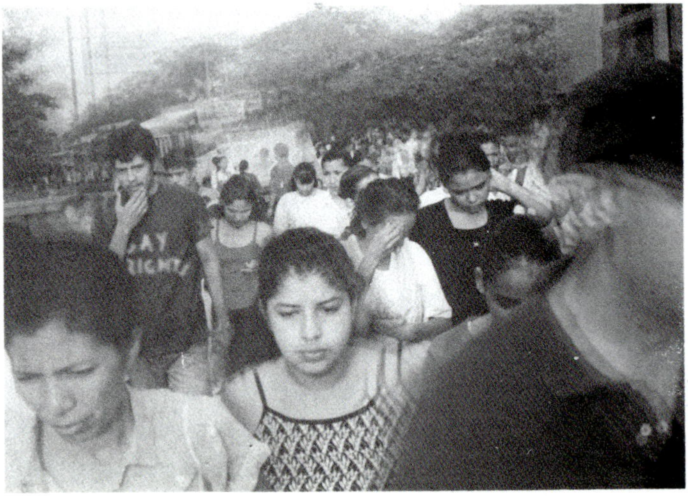

NICARAGUA has a sodomy law, punishable with up to 4 years in prison.

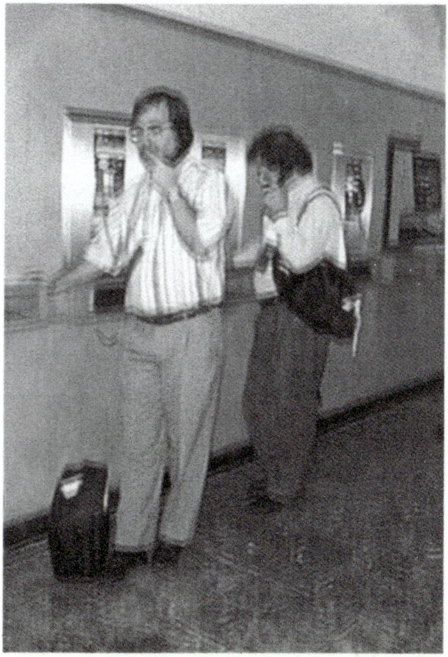

USA/Ohio: A man asking another man to have sex (seeking consent) is a First Degree Misdemeanour (Importuning Statute), 6 months in prison (7 months if the prisoner can`t pay the fine).

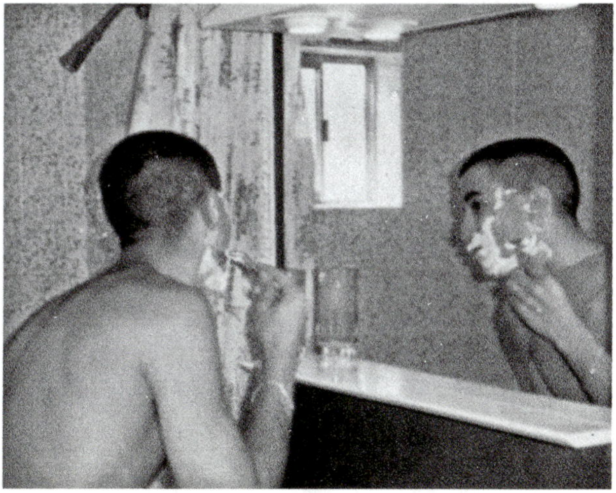

TURKEY: Homosexual activity is legal, the age of sexual consent is 18 for vaginal and anal sex, and 16 for all other sex. Homosexuals are banned from the military, and homosexual officers and conscripts must serve prison sentences of 3 to 6 months. Article 10 of the Law of Associations can be used to make gay organizations illegal.

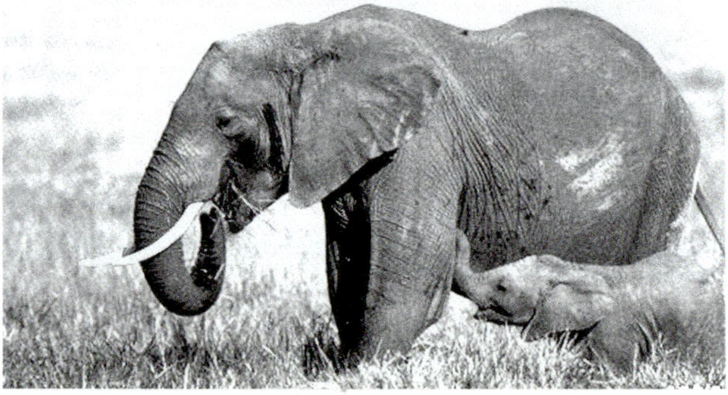

African Elephant / Asiatic Elephant
In wild African and Asiatic Elephant males, homosexual mounting is a fairly common and regular occurrence, especially among younger bulls. In addition, Asiatic Elephant males spend an average of 10 percent of their time in play-fighting (which also include mounting between males), while individual African Elephant bulls may participate in erotic combat up to 4 or five times a day during some times of the year. Approximately 18 percent of male Asiatic Elephants have a male companion. In captivity, about 11 percent of social interactions between male Asiatic Elephants involve sexual activities, compared to approximately a quarter of social interactions between females; overall, roughly 45 percent of sexual interactions involve same-sex participants.

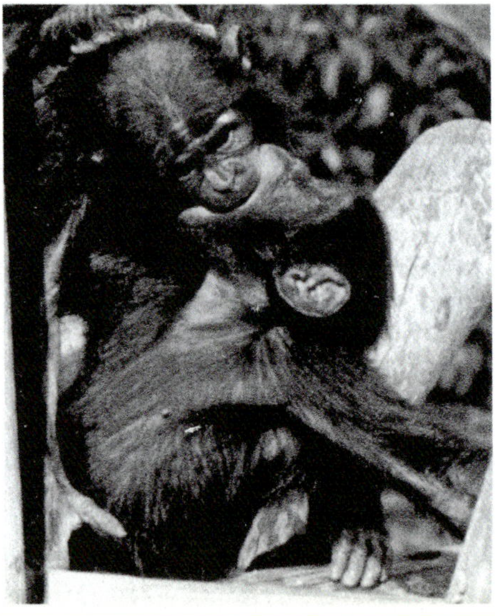

Two male Bonobos kissing.
Frequency of homosexual behaviour: Bonobo and Pygmy Chimpanzee/ Homosexual activity is nearly as common as heterosexual activity in Bonobos, accounting for 40-50% of all sexual interactions; two-thirds to three-quarters of this same-sex activity is between females.

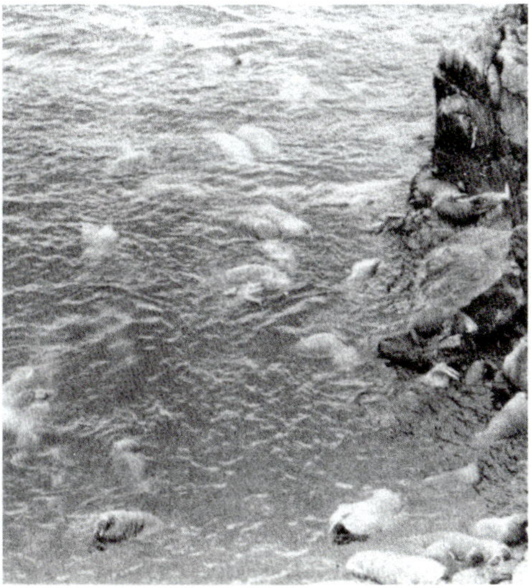

A group of male Walruses off the coast of Round Islands, Alaska. Pairs of males are participating in courtship and other activities with each other while floating in the water. Male Walruses are often seasonally bisexual, engaging in homosexual pursuits outside the breeding season.

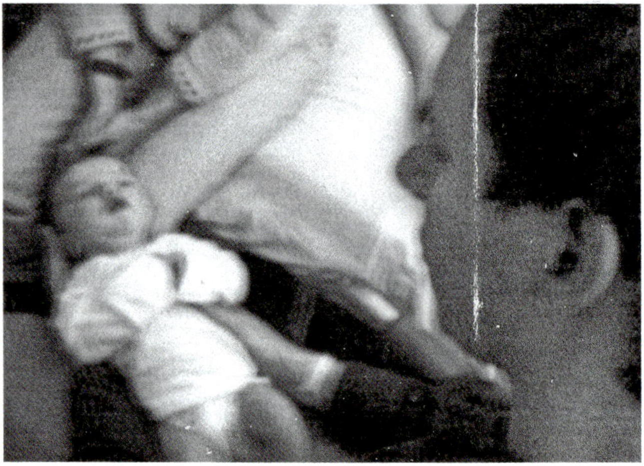

GERMANY bans artificial insemination for lesbians.

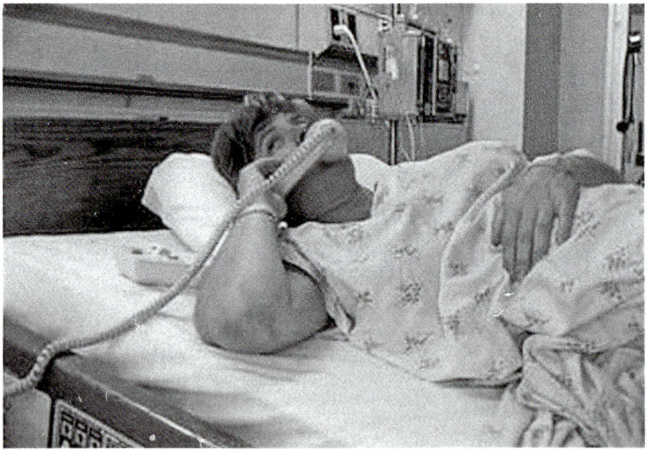

Adoption: In the United Kingdom, adoption is possible only for married couples or single persons. No reference to sexual orientation is found but homosexuals are not allowed to marry in the U.K.

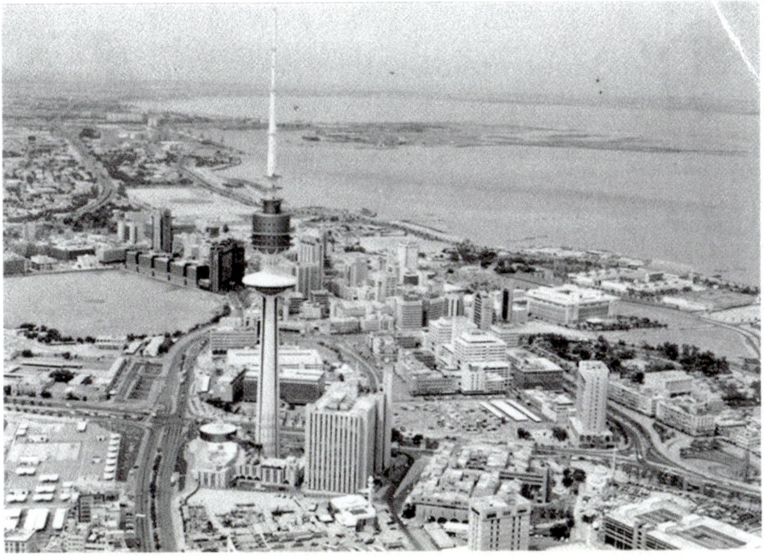

KUWAIT: Has a sodomy law, punishes sexual intercourse between men over 21 years of age with imprisonment of up of to seven years, it punishes sexual intercourse with a male under 21 with imprisonment of up to 10 years.

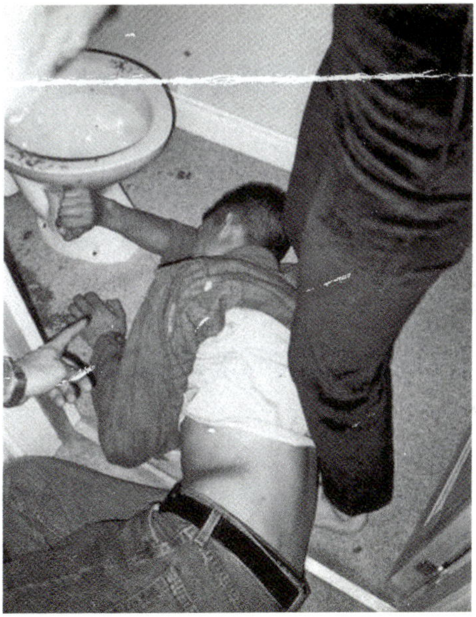

Homophobic hate crimes: Homophobic violence and bullying are a common experience for many young lesbians and gays. In 1996, in a United Kingdom survey of hate crimes against lesbian and gay men involving over 4,000 respondents, one in three gay men and one in four lesbians reported that they had experienced a violent attack in the last five years. 48% of those under 18 reported violent attacks and 50% of these attacks took place in schools and were carried out by fellow students.

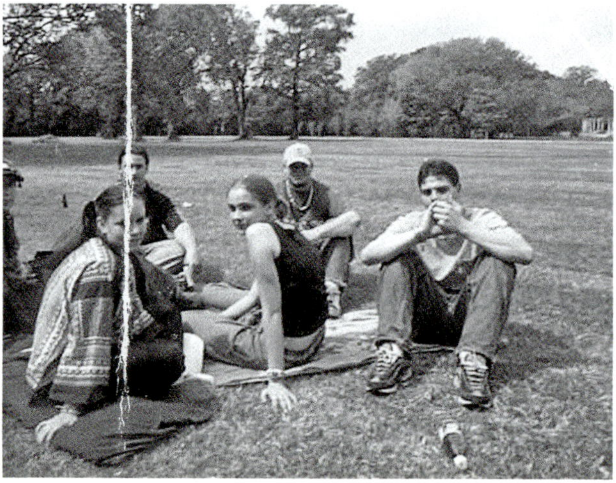

ROMANIA: Repealed it`s sodomy laws, leaving in place a provision giving 5 years in prison for homosexuals inciting a “public scandal”. A public scandal is defined as any homosexual relationship found offensive by two or more people. Bans the presentation of homosexuality in a positive light.

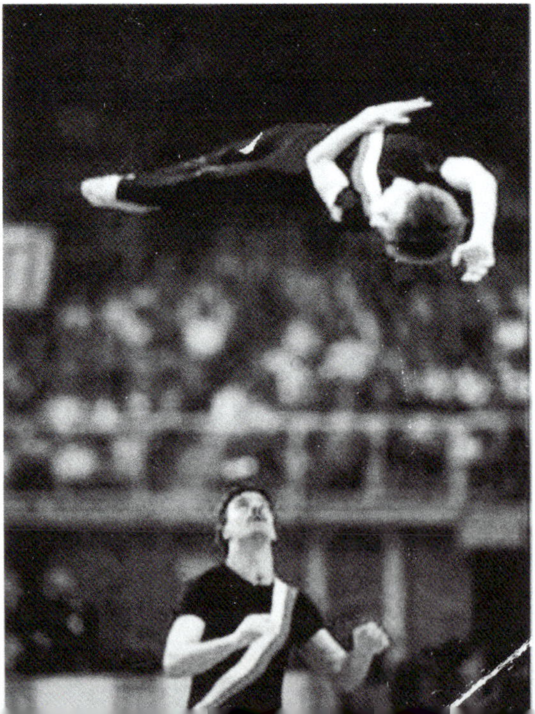

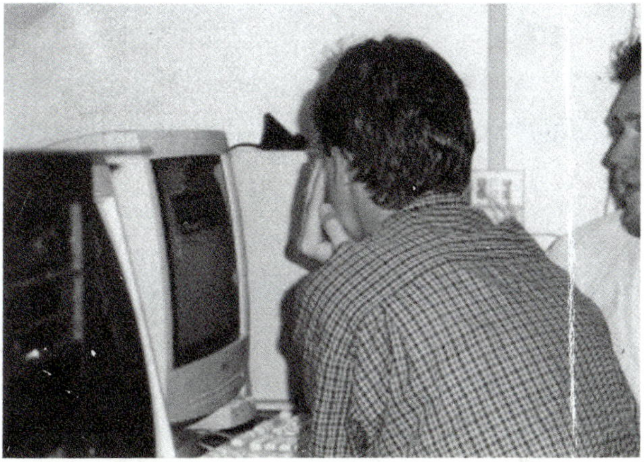

USA/North Carolina has a sodomy law: Maximum Penalty: 10 Years & Discretionary Fine.

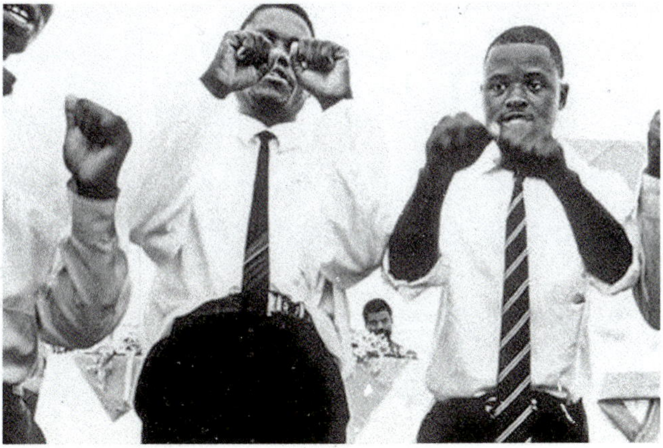

High-school pupils sing a song about AIDS in traditional Zulu choral style at an AIDS awareness event. Educating the public about AIDS has taken on many forms in Africa, from putting on dramas about AIDS for school children, to AIDS awareness card games.

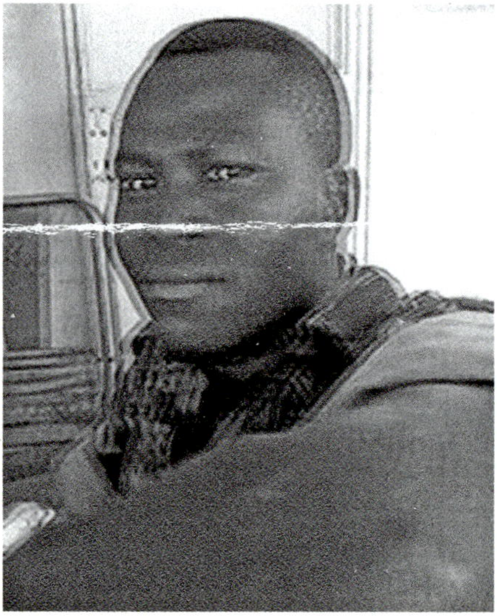

UGANDA: Homosexual activity is illegal, criminalizes "carnal knowledge against the order of nature" with a maximum penalty of life imprisonment. Section 141 prohibits "attempts at carnal knowledge" with a maximum penalty of 7 years imprisonment.

Situation of gays and lesbians and their partners in respect to asylum and immigration in the member states of the Council of Europe: Most countries claim not to have had to deal with an asylum request founded on sexual orientation.

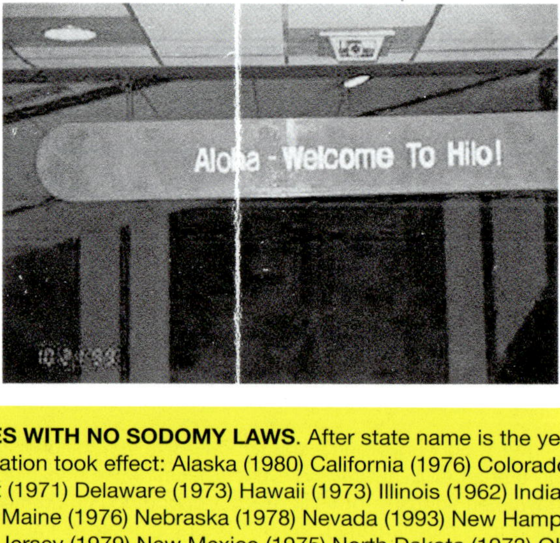

USA/STATES WITH NO SODOMY LAWS. After state name is the year the decriminalization took effect: Alaska (1980) California (1976) Colorado (1972) Connecticut (1971) Delaware (1973) Hawaii (1973) Illinois (1962) Indiana (1977) Iowa (1978) Maine (1976) Nebraska (1978) Nevada (1993) New Hampshire (1975) New Jersey (1979) New Mexico (1975) North Dakota (1973) Ohio (1974) Oregon (1972) Rhode Island (1998) South Dakota (1977) Vermont (1977) Washington (1976) West Virginia (1976) Wisconsin (1983) Wyoming (1977).

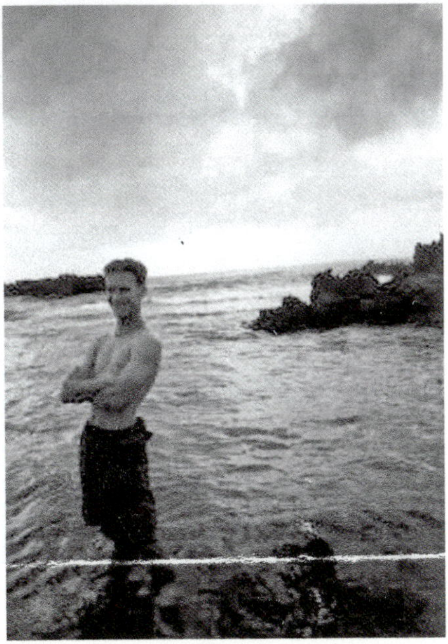

IRELAND: Has no sodomy laws, the age of sexual consent is 17 for homosexual males regarding anal and oral sex, 15 for lesbians, and for heterosexuals. Oral sex is legal at age 15. Has a national gay rights law that bans some anti-gay discrimination, including employment. Religious institutions are exempted in instances where it conflicts with their teachings. Citizens can only adopt a child if they are legally married, widowed or judicially separated people.

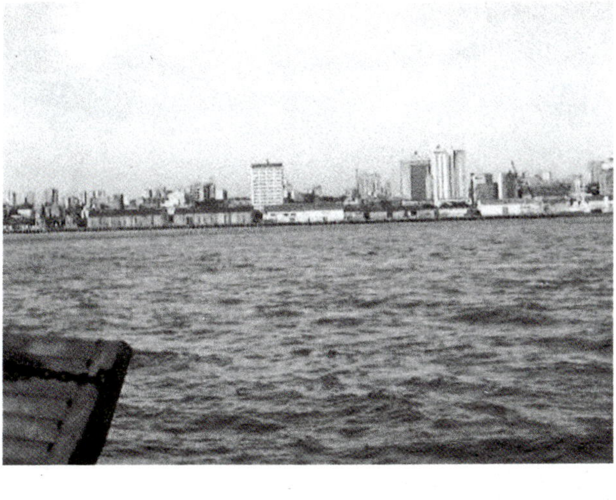

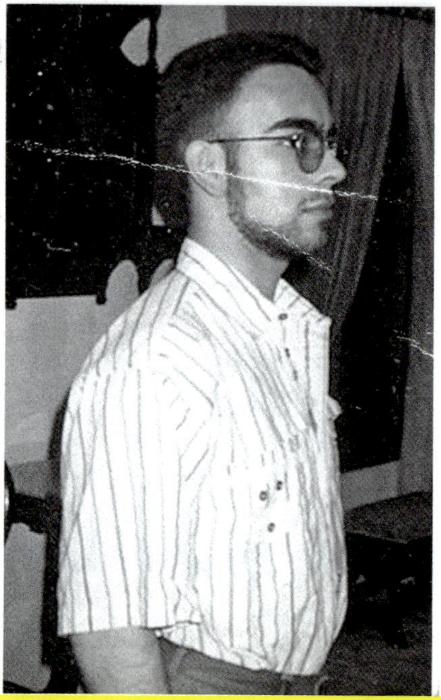

Situation in the armed forces/United Kingdom
In the United Kingdom, 600 men and women have been forced to leave the armed forces over the past ten years because of their homosexual orientation.

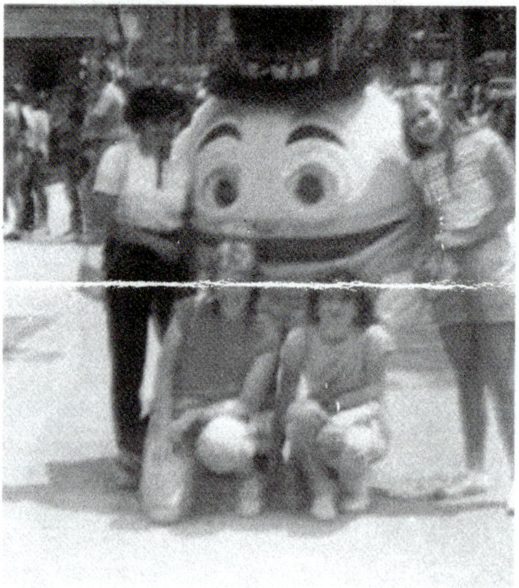

USA/Oklahoma has a sodomy law.
Maximum Penalty: 10 Years.
The law applies to Homosexuals only.

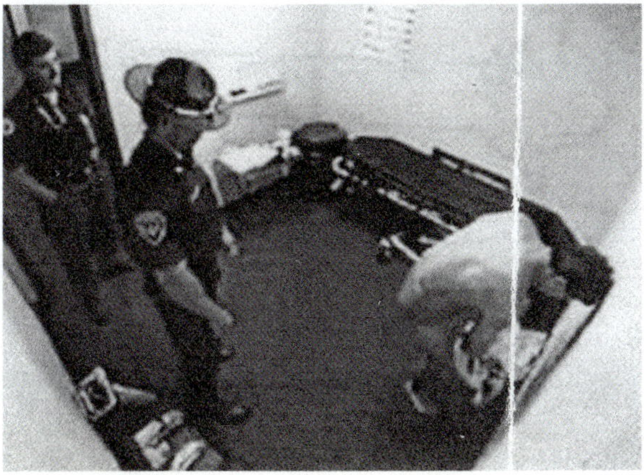

USA/Idaho has a sodomy law.
Maximum Penalty: Life In Prison.

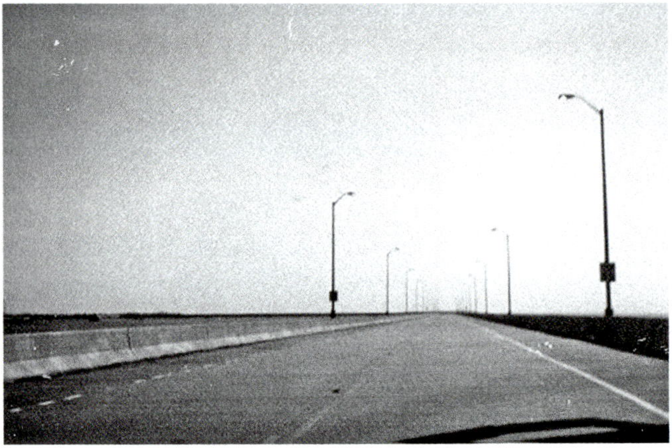

Laws on sexual offences: In many countries the age of consent for same-sex and opposite-sex sexual acts differs: Albania, Austria, Bulgaria, Croatia, Cyprus, Estonia, Hungary, Ireland, Liechtenstein, Lithuania, Moldova, Portugal, Romania and the United Kingdom.

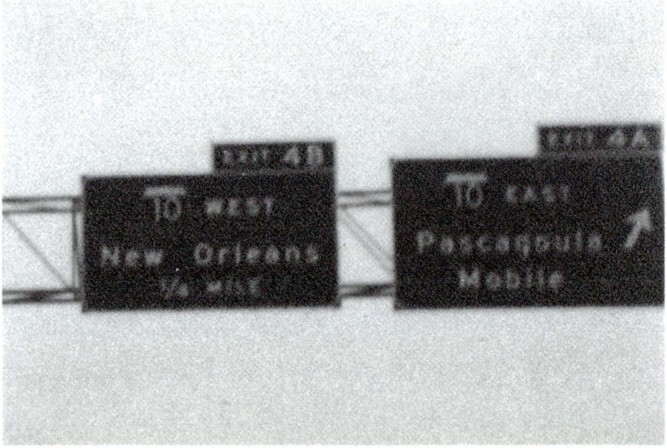

USA: Estimated gay men living with, and estimated deaths of gay men with AIDS, by year.

Year	Living	Deaths
1993	100.365	26.939
1994	109.806	28.575
1995	117.086	28.048
1996	127.110	19.248
1997	140.077	9.989
1998	152.021	7.899

source:
U.S. DEPARTMENT OF HEALTH AND HUMAN SERVICES

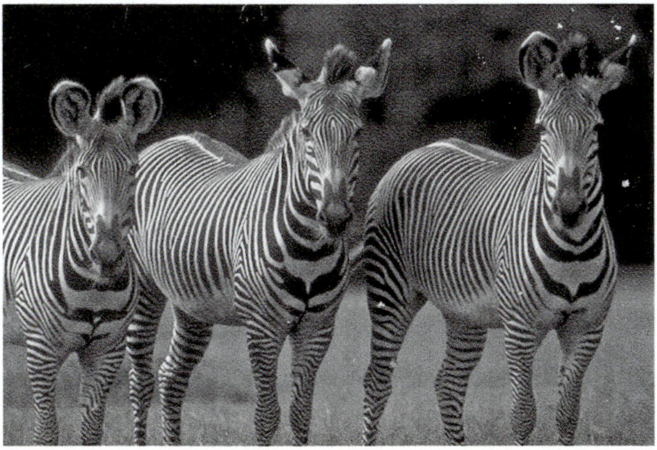

Mountain Zebra / Plains Zebra
In Captivity, mounting and attempted mounting occur in about 60 percent of interactions between male Plains Zebras. Among wild Mountain Zebras, homosexual interactions are less frequent. About 20 percent of play interactions between bachelor males involve mounting, while herd stallions associate with bachelor males about 5 percent of the time.

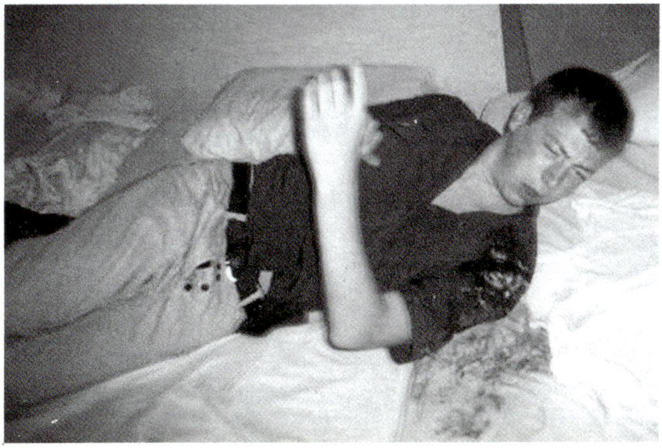

USA/Maryland: has a sodomy law
Maximum Penalty: 10 Years & $1,000.00 Fine.
The law applies to Homosexuals only.

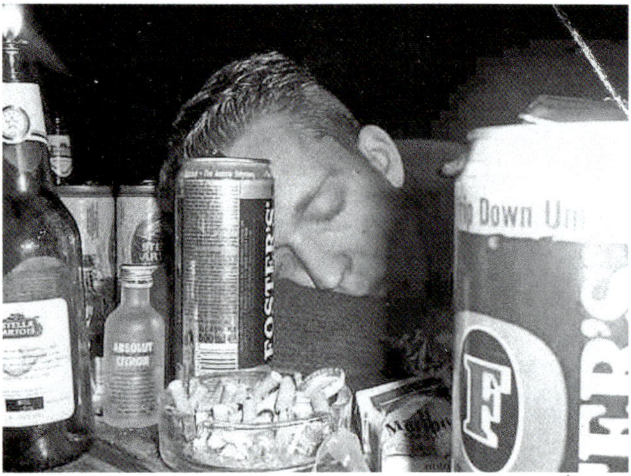

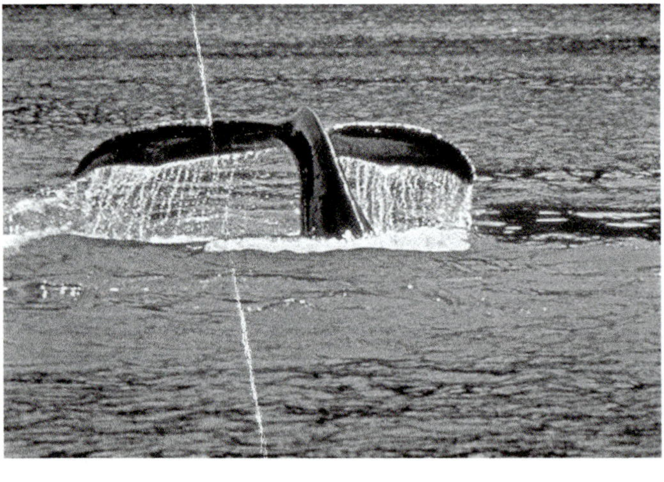

Frequency of homosexual behaviour among gray whales:
At least a quarter of all companion pairs are same-sex.

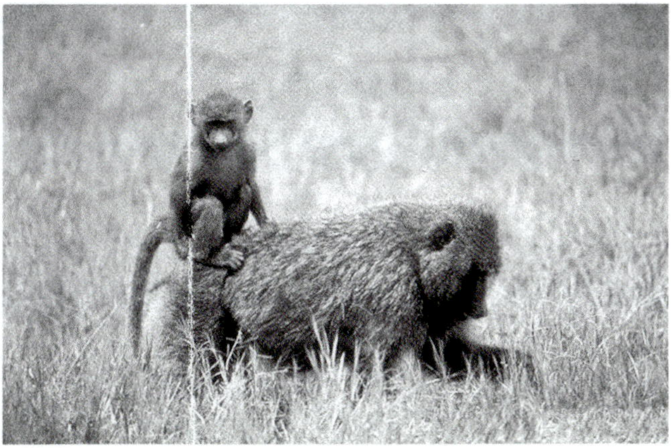

Frequency of homosexual behaviour among apes:
Bonobos/ Pygmy Chimpanzee: 40-50% - Common Chimpanzee: 29-33% - Gorillas: Male 7-36% Females 9-14% - Orang-Utan: 9%

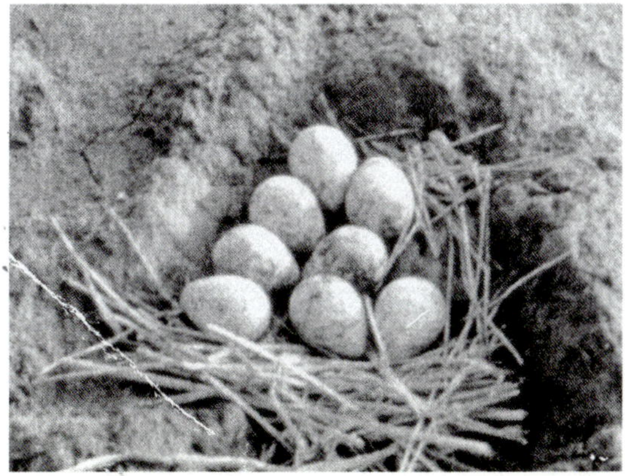

Frequency of homosexual behaviour among birds:
Greylang Goose: 14% - Canada Goose: 12% - Snow Goose 4% - Black Swan: 5-20% - Mallard Duck: 2-19% - Flamingo: 5-6%

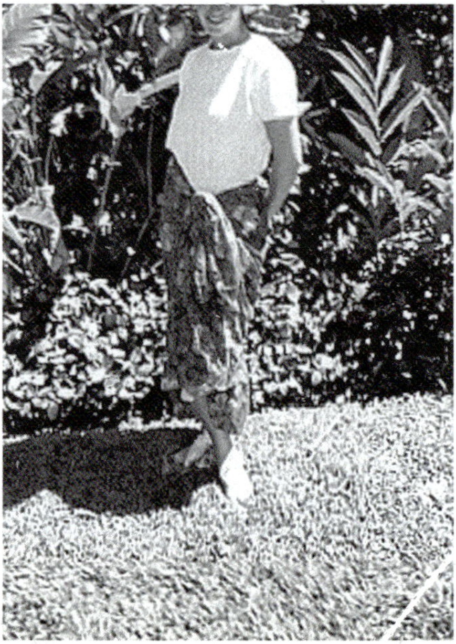

FIJI has a sodomy law, punishable with up to 14 years in prison, with or without corporal punishment.

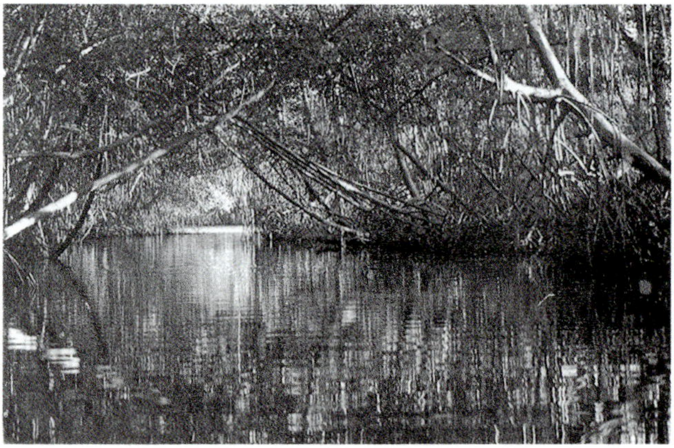

TRINIDAD AND TOBAGO has a sodomy law, punishable with 10 to 20 years in prison. It provides a penalty of up to life imprisonment if committed on a minor (under 18 years old). Under Article 8 of the Immigration Act, homosexuals are not allowed to enter the country.

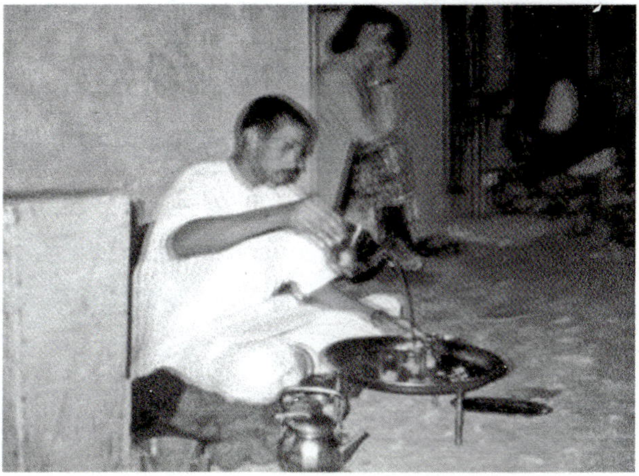

MAURITANIA has a sodomy law, punishable with death.

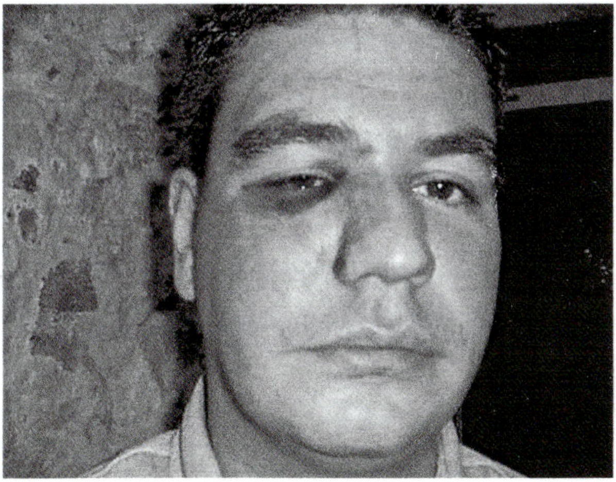

Homophobic hate crimes: In 1996, in a United Kingdom survey of hate crimes against lesbian and gay men involving over 4000 respondents, one in three gay men and one in four lesbians reported that they had experienced a violent attack in the last five years. The scale of the violence was often very extreme and included stabbing, shootings, severe beatings, rape and assault.

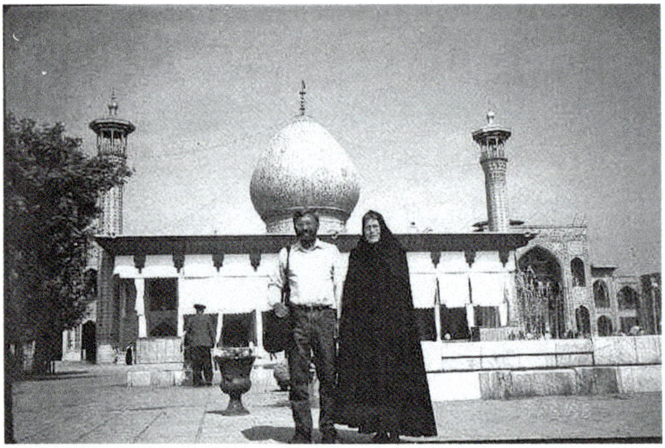

COUNTRIES WHERE HOMOSEXUAL ACTS ARE PUNISHABLE BY DEATH:
Afghanistan, Iran, Mauritania, Pakistan, Saudi Arabia, Sudan, Yemen.

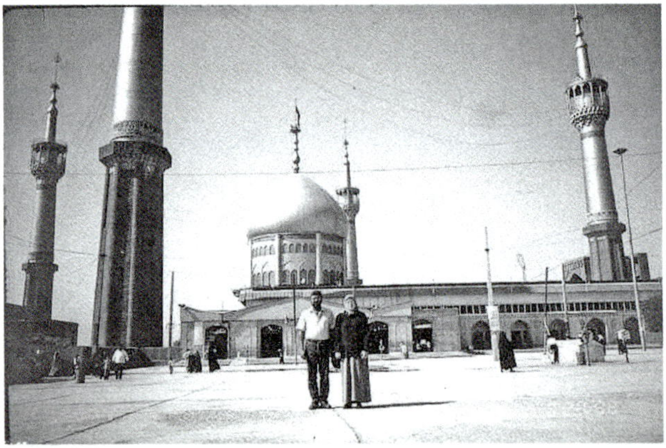

In approximately 40 countries around the world same-sex relationships, whether between men or women, remain illegal, while in a further approximately 40 countries, same-sex sexual relationships between men only also remain illegal. In at least 7 countries the maximum penalty is death.

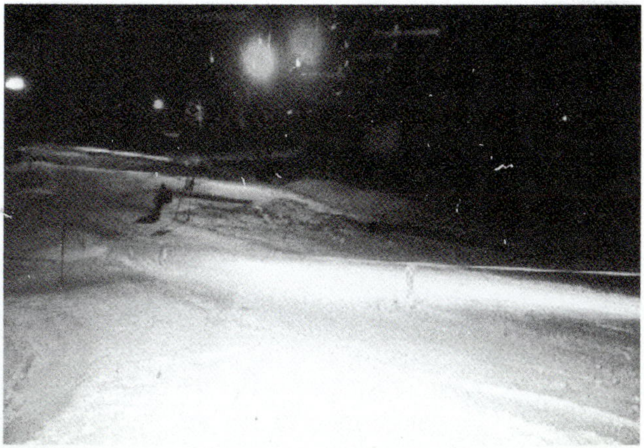

USA/Arkansas. (March 31, 2001)
"Ten guys were arrested this week for cruising here. One of the TV stations led the news with a story and listed names of the guys arrested. Then repeated the story again the next evening, focusing on two that were teachers. The cop interviewed said they would continue sending undercover cops to the mall. The Arkansas Democrat-Gazette
newspaper ran an article."

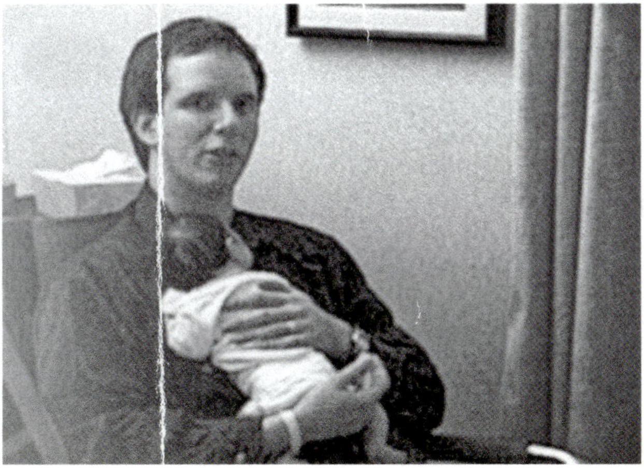

Adoption: In Spain, adoption by a homosexual couple is not possible under the legislation as the law provides that nobody may be adopted by more than one person except a married couple.
Plentiful research has been conducted on this subject over the last twenty years. None of it has established that children could have suffered a handicap through being brought up by homosexual parents, or that they are worse parents than heterosexual ones, or that such children are any more likely to become homosexuals themselves.

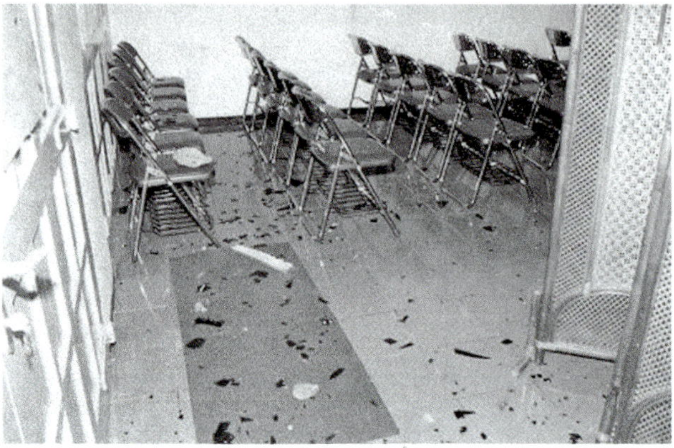

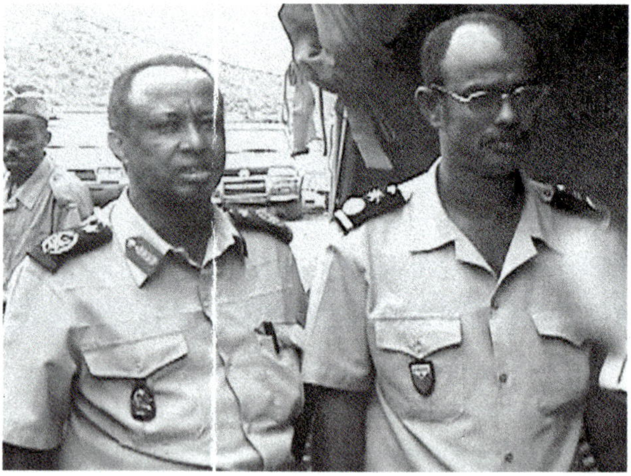

SOMALIA has a sodomy law, punished with imprisonment from 3 months to 3 years, and an act of lust different from sexual intercourse is punished with imprisonment from 2 months to 2 years.

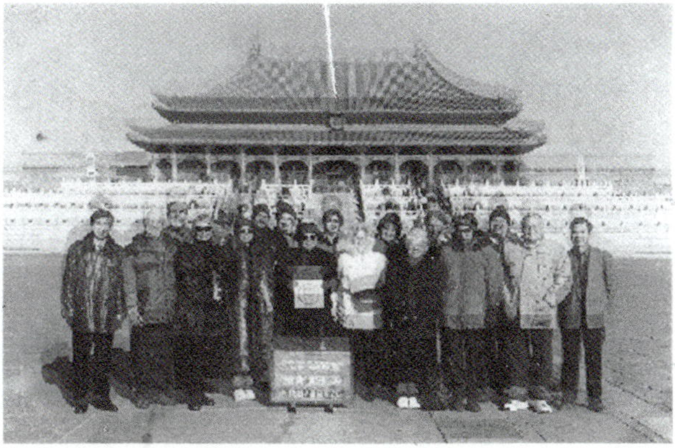

The Government of China estimated that at the end of 1996 up to 200,000 people were living with HIV/AIDS. This figure was doubled by the end of 1997. There are two major epidemics under way in China. One is in injecting drug users in the mountainous Southwest of the country. The other, newer epidemic is now surfacing among heterosexuals, especially along the prosperous eastern seaboard where prostitution is re-emerging as the gap grows between rich and poor. The warning signs of high-risk behaviour are worryingly clear: sexually transmitted diseases (STDs) have shot up in recent years, and there are no suggestions that the trend will be broken.

Source: UNAIDS Joint United Nations Programme on HIV/AIDS, "AIDS Epidemic Update December 2000" and "Report on the global HIV/AIDS epidemic June 2000"

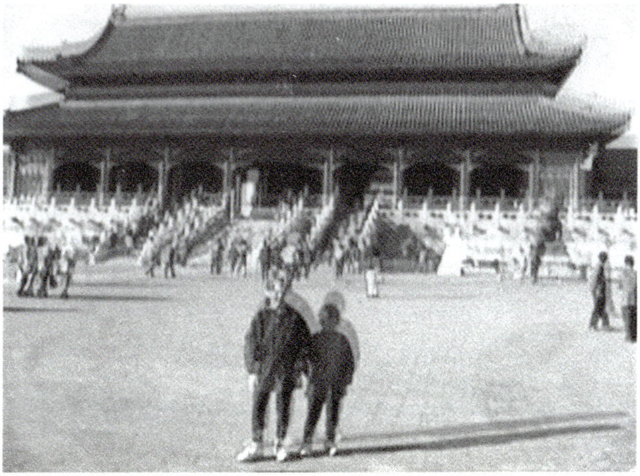

CHINA has no sodomy laws.

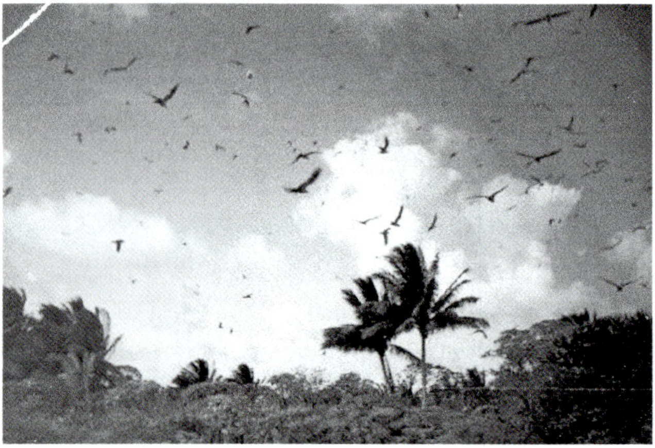

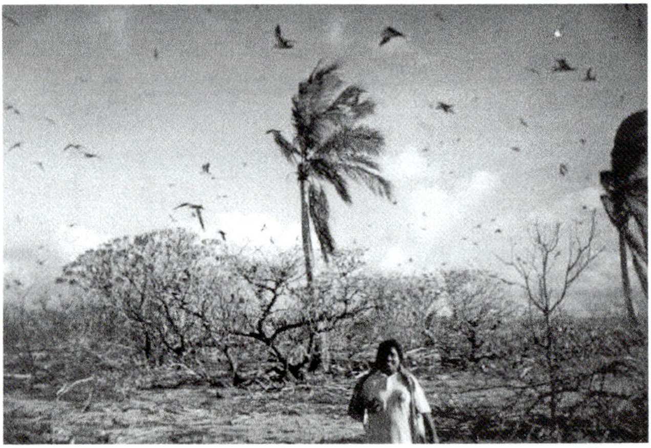

KIRIBATI has a sodomy law, punishable with up to 14 years in prison.

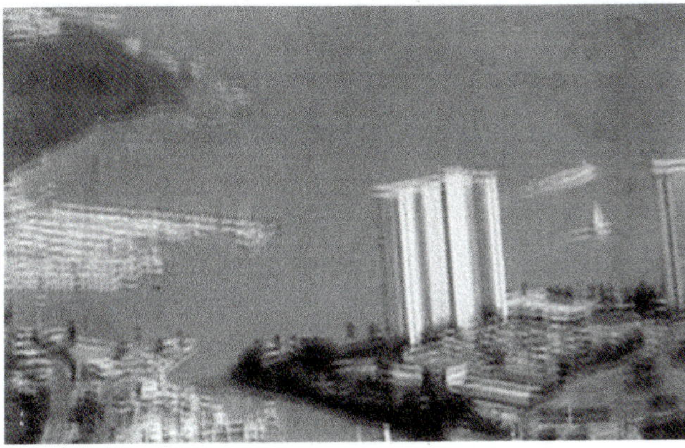

PUERTO RICO has a sodomy law, punished with up to 10 years in prison.

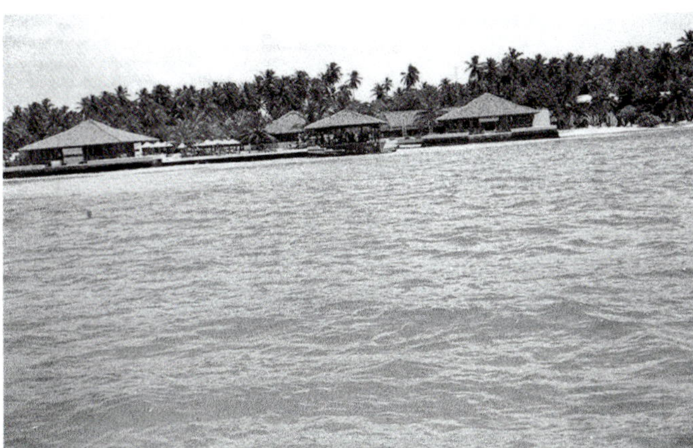

MALDIVES: Male homosexual sex is forbidden by law, punishable with a maximum sentence of life in prison.

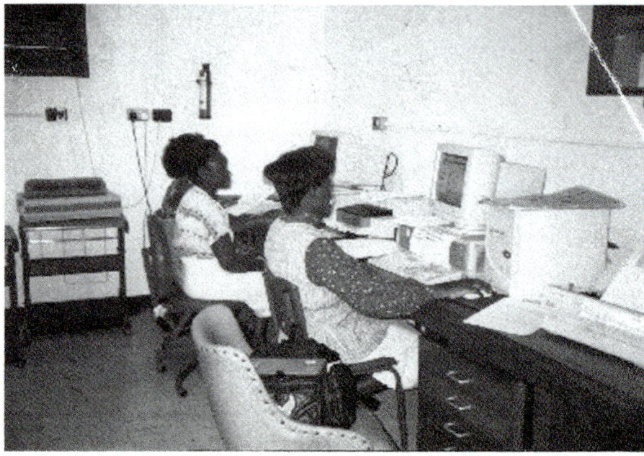

ZIMBABWE: Homosexual activity is illegal, punishable by up to 10 years in prison.

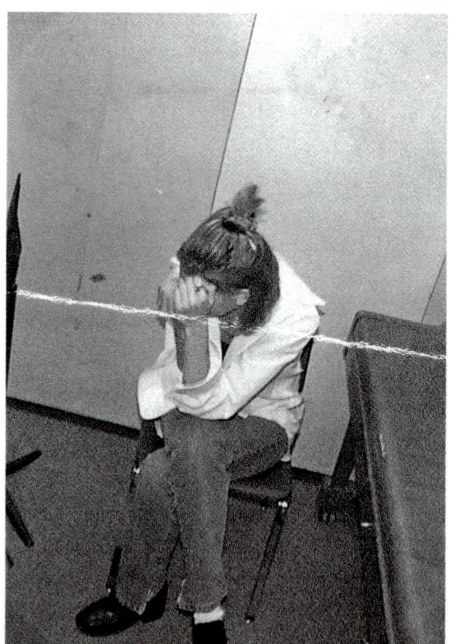

USA/Arkansas has a sodomy law:
Maximum Penalty: 1 Year & $1,000.00 Fine.
The law applies to Homosexuals only.

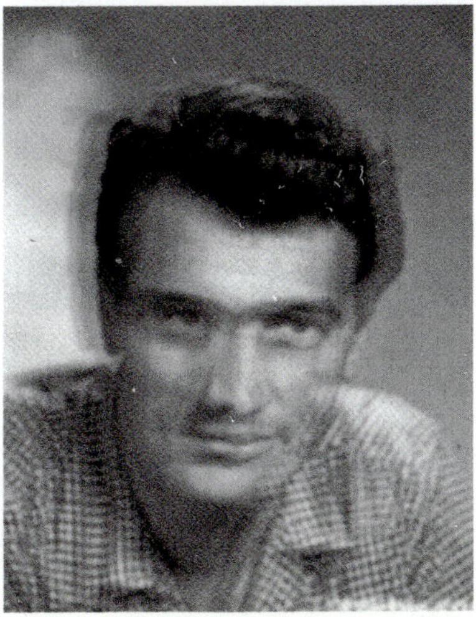

Already, 18.8 million people around the world have died of AIDS, 3.8 million of them children. Nearly twice that many - 34.3 million - are now living with HIV, and most of these are likely to die over the next decade or so.
The most recent estimates show that, in 1999 alone, 5.3 million people were newly infected with HIV.

Source: UNAIDS Joint United Nations Programme on HIV/AIDS, "AIDS Epidemic Update December 2000" and "Report on the global HIV/AIDS epidemic June 2000"

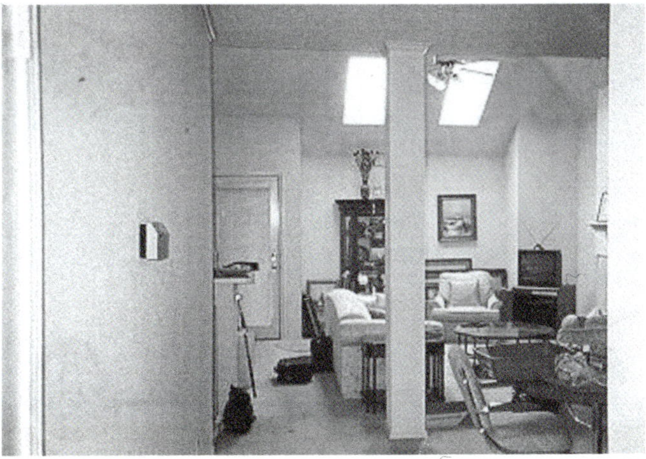

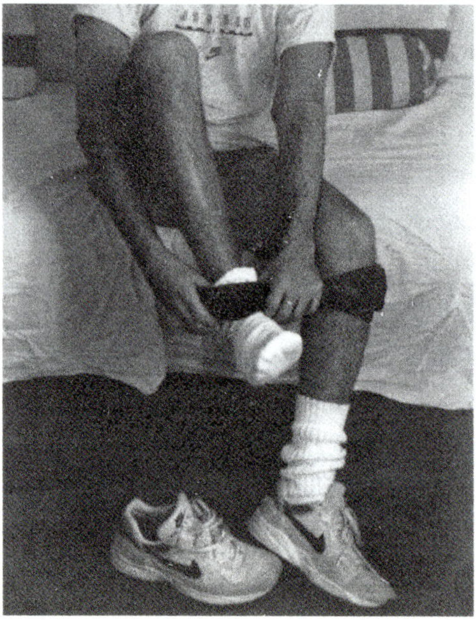

ALBANIA has no sodomy laws, the age of sexual consent is 18 for homosexual males, and 14 for lesbians and heterosexuals.

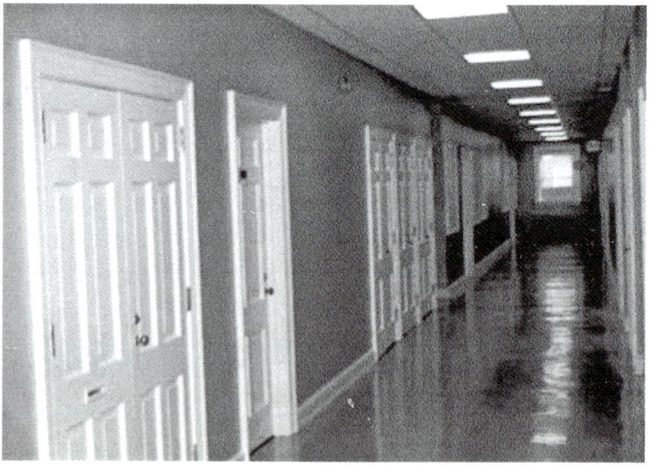

LIECHTENSTEIN has no sodomy laws, the age of sexual consent is 18 for homosexuals and 14 for lesbians and heterosexuals. Formation of lesbian and gay organizations is prohibited. Promotion of homosexuality is prohibited.

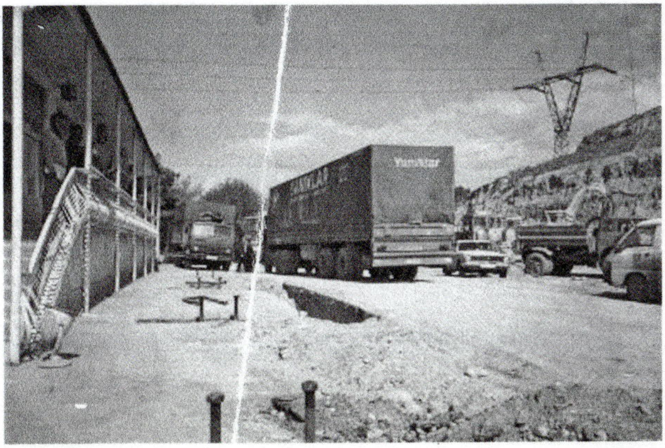

AZERBAIJAN has a sodomy law, punishable with 5 to 7 years in prison for anal sex. Oral sex is legal. Lesbian sex is not mentioned in the law.

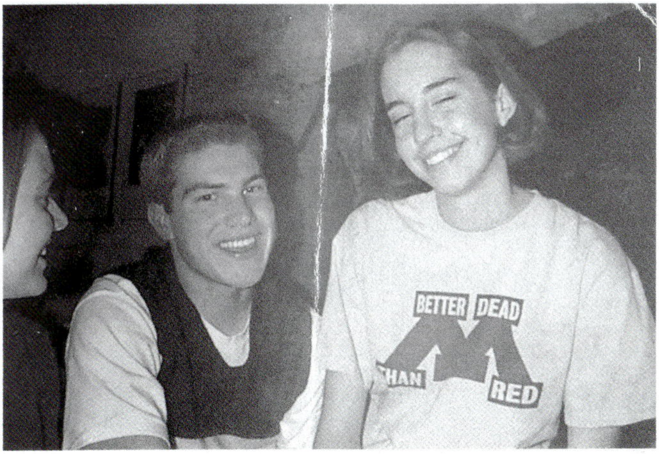

USA/Michigan has a sodomy law:
Maximum Penalty: 15 Years
(Repeat Offenders: Life In Prison).

KONTEXT is a series by DISTANZ.

Acknowledgements

Many thanks to Kirsty Bell, Daniel Buchholz and Christopher Müller, Sonia Fernández Pan, Lorena Juan and Lena Zimmermann.

A special thanks goes to Marc Siegel and the Estate of Douglas Crimp.

A special thanks goes to Henrik Olesen.

Colophon

Editor
Matthias Kliefoth

Design
Ingo Maak
Manuel Tayarani

Proofreading
Rebecca Wilton

Image Editing
max color, Berlin

Production Management
Rebecca Wilton

Printing and Binding
medialis Offsetdruck GmbH, Berlin

Copyrights and courtesy
Elliot Erwitt courtesy Magnum Photos, New York and Agentur Focus, Hamburg
Peter Hujar courtesy The Peter Hujar Archive, Pace Gallery, New York
and Fraenkel Gallery San Fransisco
Henrik Olesen courtesy Galerie Buchholz, Köln/Berlin/New York

Distribution
Edel Germany GmbH
international-books@edel.com

ISBN 978-3-95476-357-3

Printed in Germany

Published by
DISTANZ Verlag
www.distanz.de